new **china**
architecture

by XING RUAN   photography by PATRICK BINGHAM-HALL

PERIPLUS

Published by Periplus Editions (HK) Ltd., with editorial
offices at 130 Joo Seng Road #06-01 Singapore 368357

ISBN 0-7946-0389-0

Distributed by:
North America, Latin America & Europe
Tuttle Publishing
364 Innovation Drive
North Clarendon, VT 05759-9436
Tel: (802) 773 8930
Fax: (802) 773 6993
Email: info@tuttlepublishing.com
www.tuttlepublishing.com

Japan
Tuttle Publishing
Yaekari Building, 3F, 5-4-12 Osaki
Shinagawa-ku, Tokyo 141-0032
Tel: (813) 5437 0171
Fax: (813) 5437 0755
E-mail: tuttle-sales@gol.com

Asia Pacific
Berkeley Books Pte Ltd
130 Joo Seng Road #06-01
Singapore 368357
Tel: (65) 6280 1330
Fax: (65) 6280 6290
E-mail: inquiries@periplus.com.sg
www.periplus.com

Printed in Singapore

10 09 08 07 06 5 4 3 2 1

Page 1 photograph: Faculty of Architecture and Civil
Engineering, Shenzhen University
Shenzhen 2003
Architect – Gong Weimin

Page 2 image: China Central Television (CCTV)
Headquarters
Beijing 2008 (estimated completion date)
Architect – Rem Koolhaas and OMA

Right: Suitcase House
Commune by the Great Wall, Shui Guan 2001
Architect – Gary Chang

contents

Left: Airport House
Commune by the Great Wall, Shui Guan 2001
Architect – Chien Hsueh-Yi

A Hundred Flowers

Discerning the 'Good' in China's Modern Architecture

'Flowering'

Much has changed since the publication of 'Great Leap Forward' in 2001,[1] a Harvard University research project coordinated by Rem Koolhaas, on the urbanization of China's Pearl River Delta. One thing that has remained unchanged though, and is indeed much inflated, is the enormous interest in China shown by the West. The popularity enjoyed by the 'Great Leap Forward' has been followed by various special issues of architectural journals focusing on new architecture in China, notably the December 2003 feature issue – 'Architecture in China' – of the Japanese A + U (Architecture and Urbanism), with an editorial entitled 'The Flowering of Chinese Architecture', and the March 2004 special issue – 'China Builds with Superhuman Speed, Reinventing its Cities from the Ground Up' – of the American Architectural Record, which also saw a Chinese version released in collaboration with the Tongji University of Shanghai. Every such publication, needless to say, is a framed view – a 'pair of spectacles' – with a subjective selection of projects. The Koolhaas project, to generalize, has a taste for the enormity of the scale and speed of China's urbanization;[2] it is also spiced, due to a distaste for the coarse and raw realities of this urbanization, with an excessive use of blurry and digitized images of the bastardized architectural and urban kitsch. Recent publications show a different appetite for the 'new', and large plates of professional photographs are surprising people, alerting them to the circumstance whereby China is now able to achieve what the West saw in the 20th century – only bigger and better.

To some extent, this book – 'New China Architecture' – belongs to the latter, but with a different agenda. On the one hand, it attempts to provide a sense of realism, seen in the context of my own historical background, which, though nonetheless biased, was a 'bodily' understanding (the author grew up in the second half of the 20th century in China, and was an unworthy peer of some of the architects included in this book); but on the other hand, a knowing sense of irony is embedded in the text, while the glamorous accompanying images are deciphered. To paraphrase the theme of the A+U feature issue, my hope is that the paradox of 'reality' and 'fiction' will inspire the readers to pick the 'flowers' from the 'weeds'. The book is a snapshot, but the larger aim of the snapshot is to provide a starting point for the readers to gain further understanding of not only these buildings, but also the circumstances under which these buildings are produced.

The general tones of recent publications, with no exception, celebrate the unprecedented diversity of China's emerging new architecture. The Chinese words *baihua qifang*, meaning 'letting a hundred flowers blossom', are, for example, printed

Jinmao Tower
Shanghai 1997-1999
Architect – Skidmore Owings and Merrill;
East China Architectural Design and Institute

Beijing Books Building
Beijing 2008 (estimated completion date)
Architect - Rem Koolhaas and OMA

on the flowering pinkish cover of the A + U special issue. *Baihua qifang* as an expression is familiar to all in China, for it was the most publicized art policy of Chairman Mao Zedong. In 1957 he famously declared:

"Letting a hundred flowers blossom and a hundred schools of thought contend is the policy for promoting the progress of the arts and the sciences and a flourishing socialist culture in our land. Different forms and styles in art should develop freely and different schools in science should contend freely. We think that it is harmful to the growth of art and science if administrative measures are used to impose one particular style of art or school of thought and to ban another. Questions of right and wrong in the arts and sciences should be settled through free discussion in artistic and scientific circles and through practical work in these fields. They should be settled in summary fashion." [3]

Ironically though, prosperity and diversity did not materialize until long after Mao's death in 1976. So what exactly is this unprecedented architectural 'flowering' in China? A cartoonist's collage of three 'mega' cities – Beijing, Shanghai and Guangzhou – offers a glimpse: iconic buildings, most of them built in the past decade, from each city are juxtaposed with only an elevated freeway to separate them (figure 1). The scene is, on the one hand, compellingly real, for each city and its buildings are easily recognizable, for in addition to the old landmarks such as the Great Wall near Beijing, the Bund in Shanghai and the Five-Goat Statue in Guangzhou, the new iconic buildings are equally, if not more, visible. They include Paul Andreu's National Grand Theater in Beijing, SOM's Jinmao Tower, and KPF's World Financial Center in Shanghai (all by foreign architects). Yet, on the other hand, the vision is surreal, as if the buildings in these cities were displayed like animals in a zoo.

My sense is that anyone who sees this three-city collage would smile, but really one does not quite know how to react to it, as what at first may seem to be amusing could quickly evoke a slight sense of melancholy. Not only intellectuals, but also capitalists, must at some point worry about this 'unbearable lightness of being' (to paraphrase Milan Kundera), caused by an architectural 'zoo' contest that may well lead towards a drain of our limited environmental resources, and subsequently provoke an uncontrollable, monstrous explosion. To compound this speculation, we only need to consider a few statistics: the Three Gorges hydro-electrical dam construction cost $US24.65 billion, and the 488-meter high World Financial Center under construction in Shanghai (take a note of the auspicious double-eight digits) will cost $US825 million. Shanghai, a city with a population of approximately 20 million (the same as that of Australia), has more than 2800 high-rise buildings above 18 storeys, and there

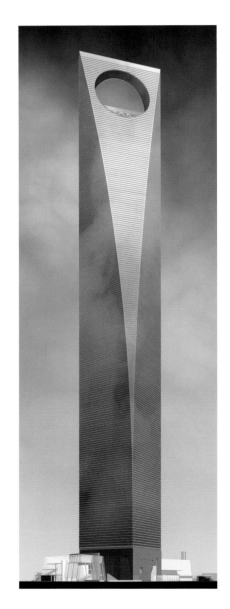

Shanghai World Financial Center
Shanghai 1994-
Architect - Kohn Pedersen Fox Associates

Looped Hybrid Housing
Beijing 2003 -
Architect – Steven Holl

are approximately 2000 more towers about to go up. China's current total annual expenditure in building construction is about $US375 billion, which adds up to 16% of the country's total GDP, and in a global perspective, China now consumes 54.7% of the world's total cement production, 36.1% of the steel and 30.4% of the coal. As for the future statistics, we only need to consider the scale of China's urbanization in the next 20 years, when it is estimated that there will be 200 million farmers moving from the country to the city.

But far worse, for the intellectuals, would be that the splendid built world may be achieved at the expense of a potential collapse of the moral edifice. What then is the 'Good', in the sense of how Iris Murdoch might have phrased it?[4] We naturally assume that this sort of 'delirious lightness' (more than Kundera's 'unbearable lightness'), mainly caused by the sheer speed and quantity of China's urban and architectural progress, is unprecedented. But let us pause, and look into history…

'In late medieval France, collective pride took the form of building the tallest vault or spire, and Amiens and Beauvais competed with each other in foolish disregard for the laws of engineering. The vault of Beauvais Cathedral soared to 157 feet and three inches only to collapse. Pride is the deadliest sin. In raising religious edifices, the architect-engineers and their patrons demonstrated how easy it was to mask pride under the claim of glorifying God.'[5]

There is, of course, no God to be glorified in 21st century China, only capital wealth and national pride. After more than three decades of ideological battles with the West, and restrained by a stagnant state-controlled economy, the economic development of the last twenty years means, first and foremost, a long overdue affluence, which is much needed to sustain a stability for the life of the individual as well as the state: the levels of affluence and the technological developments of the West are much desired. The scale of economic development, or progress, can most easily be measured by China's urbanization and building construction. To use the exhausted but now really effective metaphor: the 'sleeping dragon' is awake!

Absence

Unlike its political ideologies and cultures, China's modern architecture never attracted much attention from the West throughout most of the 20th century. The reasons, undubitably, are complex. Despite political and ideological differences between China and the West in the second half of the 20th century, the continuing

Postcard showing Shanghai Pudong skyline, 2004

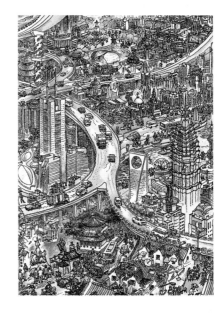

Figure 1: 'Beijing, Shanghai, Guangzhou' *by Wang Fangji,* Time + Architecture, *Shanghai: Tongji University Press, 2002-03.*

absence of China's modern architecture in Western discourse reached a remarkable, almost 'peculiar', position in the late 1990s: as China moved further away from its remote history, its new architecture somehow became more inaccessible to the West, and (so it seemed to a frustrated Chinese mind) did not even merit a footnote in Western history books, a point that will be returned to later. The situation, however, has been reversed (and how!) since 1999, when the UIA (Union of International Architects) Congress was held in Beijing. Kenneth Frampton, witnessing at first hand the headlong urbanization and a mind-boggling scale of building construction in China, implied in his UIA keynote address that he could have included more of the 'other' modern architecture – such as that of Japan, India and relatively obscure European countries – in his widely circulated *Modern Architecture: A Critical History* (1985).[6] Perhaps even to Frampton's surprise, the world's architectural media has then been racing to publish special issues on 'new architecture' in China since 1999, following the 'breakthrough' of a few young Chinese architects[7] and the attention accorded many Western architects upon winning competitions for major public buildings in China, such as those for the 2008 Beijing Olympic Games.

But until this point, the only 20th century Chinese architect known to the West was, arguably, Liang Sicheng. However, Liang, a University of Pennsylvania (hereafter abbreviated as 'Penn') graduate in 1927, made his name in the West through his research into and publications in English on China's pre-modern architecture.[8] Although predominately an architectural historian, Liang, along with Le Corbusier, Oscar Niemeyer and other eminent architects, was selected to participate in the design of the New York headquarters for the United Nations in 1947. In fact though, many of Liang's Chinese peers, the fifteen or more Chinese architects trained at Penn in the first half of the 20th century, were a major force in shaping China's modern architectural education and practice in the second half of the 20th century.[9]

These architects were trained at Penn in the 1920s under the French professor Paul Philippe Cret, and one of the most prominent architects in the group was Yang Tingbao.[10] Yang was a star pupil of Cret's, and a classmate of Louis Kahn. After returning to China, Yang became one of the most influential architects in 20th century China, and remained the spiritual leader of Chinese architectural education until his death in 1982. However, neither Yang's teaching nor his architectural work was known in the West, although the China Architecture and Building Press published *Yang Tingbao Jianzhu Zuoping Ji* (Yang Tingbao, Architectural Works and Projects) in 1983,[11] which was the first monograph ever published about an individual

Temple of Heaven, Beijing

architect in the history of China. Unfortunately, Yang did not get a chance to see his monograph, as he died just a few days before the copies were printed. This historic publication reflected, at least within China, Yang's pre-eminent position in 20th century Chinese architecture.

Despite Western familiarities with the Ecole des Beaux-Arts and its significant impact on modern architectural education and practice in China, 20th century Chinese architecture was, strangely, given an almost complete miss by Western discourse. Among the 'other' countries in the 20th century, only Japanese and (to some extent) Indian architecture have been the exceptions, in the sense that 'Eastern realities' are discoursed within the frames of 'Western theories'.[12] The 'other' and the West seem to form a symbiosis in which there are, on the one hand, common political or ideological grounds and, on the other hand, an enduring ethnographic appetite for exoticism which demands difference. Architecturally, this difference has been typically objectified as 'critical regionalism', as advocated by Kenneth Frampton.[13] In the case of Japanese architecture, the critique has moved beyond 'paper landscape, exquisite taste, and elegant, poeticized ceremony'; rather it is the appeal of modern austerity infused with Zen spirituality, exemplified in the enigmatic works of Tadao Ando.[14]

798 New Art District
Beijing 2002-

By the late 20th century, despite the increasing Western desire to interpret modern China, the lack of interest in Chinese architecture remained evident. Although the goodwill of 'cultural sensitivity' impelled a global coverage of 20th century architecture in the late editions of *Sir Banister Fletcher's A History of Architecture*, the architecture of 20th century China was included in an encyclopaedic manner.[15] In the second edition of his influential *Modern Architecture: A Critical History*, Kenneth Frampton gave more space to Japanese architecture, and added his popular chapter on "critical regionalism",[16] but the complete omission of 20th century Chinese architecture in the text does make one wonder whether China's developments are worth any serious scrutiny.[17] The absence from Western discourse of almost a century's architectural endeavour is indeed 'peculiar'... under what value system was 20th century Chinese architecture neglected altogether? Much of the 20th century Chinese architecture, unfortunately, does not seem to have matched the expectations of 'critical regionalism' (as modern architecture did in Japan or India), neither does it replicate the modern architecture of Europe and North America. The real difference is though, only in the 'look' of the architecture, for the bulk of China's modern architecture appears eclectic in style, or 'kitsch', rather than modern.[18]

Xintiandi
Shanghai 2001
Architect – Wood and Zapata; Nikken Sekkei;
Tongji University Architectural Design and
Research Institute; Skidmore Owings and Merrill

Summer Palace, Beijing

Refined Kitsch

Notwithstanding the cursory account of 20th century Chinese architecture in *Sir Banister Fletcher's A History of Architecture*, the period from the 1920s to the 1940s has been curiously treated as lacking in significance. In fact though, modern Chinese architectural education and practice took off during this period, and the Beaux-Arts tradition, which winged to China via those Chinese architects trained at Penn, has remained as an unfinished legacy ever since. Contrary to a common belief, as endorsed by Edward Said, that resistance is 'an inevitable part of acceptance' which ideas and theories must encounter when they travel to a new cultural environment, American Beaux-Arts sailed smoothly into the Chinese context in the early part of the 20th century.[19] This accidental encounter did not arouse much cultural shock, as the 'other' could be un-exotic and un-alien, and was not necessarily different.

Although these architects produced mostly quasi Beaux-Arts works that appeared eclectic in style, they were rarely bothered by problems of cultural identity, or to use a phrase of currency, 'place identity'. To them, issues of identity were merely concerned with a building's 'dress', but the essence of a building lies in its idea. My sense is that these architects searched for universal virtuosities through architectural works. The Chinese public, surprisingly, accepted the mainly Western architectural eclecticism with ease. An early 20th century urban housing type in many parts of China says more about China's voracious appetite for things Western, whilst maintaining a Chinese way of life. A townhouse typically had a masonry façade, often embellished with eclectic Western ornaments, but the spatial configuration consisted of a square courtyard enclosed by two or three-storey timber houses connected by open corridors bedecked with Chinese décor: to wit, an urbanised Chinese quadrangle house.

This happy coexistence was evident in the works of the first generation of American Beaux-Arts trained Chinese architects, and in his early career, Yang Tingbao produced fine works in a predominantly eclectic Western style. Widely regarded as a work of maturity, his Dahua Cinema in Nanjing, completed in 1935, can be seen, literally, as a civic reproduction of the above urban housing model. The exterior of the 1,070-seat cinema is that of a clean and modest Art Deco building, while the interior is designed with splendid 'Chinese Deco' (figures 2 and 3). Vagaries of taste in its ornamentation aside, the building has been in service for nearly 70 years with a fine gesture of urban courtesy, bridging the street-front to the deep interior. The Beaux-Arts axial disposition ensures a simple and smooth circulation with a theatrical double-volume lobby, which is the result of an eloquent manipulation of the grand

Figure 2: Exterior of Dahua cinema in Nanjing by Yang Tingbao, 1935, from Yang Tingbao jianzhu sheji zuoping ji, 94.

Figure 3: Lobby of Dahua cinema in Nanjing by Yang Tingbao, 1935, from Yang Tingbao jianzhu sheji zuoping ji, 95

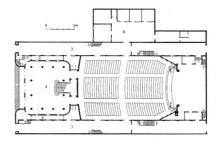

Figure 4: Ground-floor plan of Dahua cinema in Nanjing by Yang Tingbao, 1935, from Yang Tingbao jianzhu sheji zuoping ji, 96.

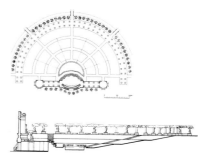

West Lake Southern Line Pavilions
Hangzhou 2002
Architect – Zhang Zi and Zhang Ming,
Original Design Studio

staircase, a colonnade, rooms and upper level balconies, based on a symmetrical axial arrangement (figure 4). Judging by its 'look', the Dahua Cinema is by no means visually avant-garde, but it is, nonetheless, a piece of refined kitsch.

Another work of Yang's shows a seamless fit between East and West, not so much in style, but rather, with the idea. In 1932, Yang built, what is known in Chinese as a 'Musical Stage' (in fact an amphitheatre), near Sun Yat-Sen's Mausoleum in Nanjing's 'Purple-Golden' Mountain area (Zijing Shan). The idea of an amphitheatre, in which the audiences sit on the ground in the open air, is arguably an idea alien to the Chinese. Yang configured the natural slope of the site as a fan-shaped sitting area, with the lawn and the hard surfaces logically juxtaposed in radiation (figure 5). The cloud-shaped stage and its masonry screen, which are adorned with 'Chinese Deco', are explicitly oriental. But more intriguing is the idea of the 'moon pond' in front of the stage, which collects the storm water, nourishes gold fish and lotus, and splashes water out from fountains. The reinforced concrete structure is hidden behind the rough-textured terrazzo plaster, which weathered quickly to give the ensemble a look of antiquity. Now, nearly three quarters of a century later, plants have graciously invaded the pergola, and soot and rainwater have dyed the 'artificial stone' surface so as it appears real (figure 6). This work – it gets better as it ages – begs the question of the 'Good' in architecture under the overarching modernity of our time.

Figure 5: Plan and cross section of the 'Musical Stage' in Nanjing by Yang Tingbao,1932, from Yang Tingbao jianzhu sheji zuoping ji, 77

Figure 6: Pergola invaded by plants in 'Musical Stage' in Nanjing by Yang Tingbao,1932, from Yang Tingbao jianzhu sheji zuoping ji, 81

In fact, the eclectic 'look' of kitsch can be completely overtaken by the grandeur of an idea: in the 1950s, driven by a self-imposed mission to revitalize China's pre-modern architecture, and indeed mixed with an optimism for the new Communist government, Liang Sicheng and his UK trained colleague Chen Zhanxiang proposed to build the new government administration offices outside old Beijing to its west, thereby saving the integrity of the imperial city. The idea was rejected by the impatient government and by future-orientated technocrats, both of whom wanted to expand Tiananmen Square to be the world's largest, and to build grand-scale monumental buildings within the ancient city fabric. As a last resort, Liang Sicheng hoped that the least the new regime could do was to save the magnificent city wall (dating back to 1264, when the Yuan dynasty began to build its imperial capital) by turning it into a civic park for the leisure life of the citizens of the new era (figure 7). Indulged by his hopeless romanticism, Liang Sicheng wanted to give the new republic capital a splendid 'green necklace' of 25 miles in length, for the city wall that enclosed imperial Beijing would now be greened by lawns and plants. This would be the world's only city ring 'park in the sky', as it was not only to be a civic place, but

Figure 7: The city-wall-park proposed by Liang Sicheng, 1951, from Wang Jun, Chengji, 110, Beijing: Shenghuo. Dushu. Xingzhi, 2003

Ningbo Urban Museum
Ningbo 2003
Architect – MADA spam

would also serve the fine Chinese habit of 'climbing high to inspect the horizon'. Had the proposal materialized, I would like to think that generations of new citizens could have been cultivated with a rare civic idealism, for the idea of civic life and place have scarcely existed in China's imperial history of many thousands of years. Who would then care about its hybrid kitsch look? The plan looks, if anything, heroically cosmopolitan.

Legend has it that Chairman Mao Zedong stood on the Tiananmen (the Gate of Heavenly Peace) facing a sea of red flags at the birth of the new republic, and visualized a forest of tall industrial chimneys on Beijing's horizon with black smoke coming out of them. Liang Sicheng was devastated! The government then tore down the entire city wall to give way to roads, an act which was seen as a symbol of industrialization, and indeed modernity. This essay of course is not the place to ventilate any bitterness, but I tend to think that Liang Sicheng's fate, dying impoverished and regretful, is not merely a consequence of the brutal regime during his lifetime, but also of the image of modernity, which has trivialized the idea – and the essence.

The architectural refinement of the first half of the 20th century in China was indeed based on essence and idea, not image. 'Modernity', seen as the equivalent of Westernization in China, was a topic of much debate in the early part of 20th century. Liang Qichao, Liang Sicheng's father, was a significant intellectual voice who advocated the idea of essence and selection. His idea of *tiyong* (more fully expressed in Chinese as *zhongxue wei ti, xixue wei yong*) suggested that Chinese learning should be the essence, while Western learning is good only for utility. Neither his son Liang Sicheng, nor Yang Tingbao, as we have already seen, took this literally. The 'double face' of Yang's Dahua Cinema, for example, is more than a crude juxtaposition of 'Western face' and 'Chinese essence'. Curiously, the columns in the lobby, painted with Chinese patterns, are neither of Chinese nor Western classical orders. The capitals of these columns are based on those of the Egyptian Temple of Isis on the Island of Philae (332 B.C. – 1st century A. D.) *(figure 3)*. Liang Junior's idea of the Beijing city wall 'sky-park' is surely a rich fermentation of both ideas and images, and these examples were meaningful and legible ideas: they are outcomes of selection and judgement of the 'Good'. For most of the 20th century, the West may have neglected the essence of refined kitsch in China, for the image of modernity in 20th century architecture has largely preferred the 'look' of austerity, rather than the idea of cosmopolitanism.

Figure 8: National Grand Theater
Beijing 2006 (estimated completion date)
Architect – Paul Andreu

Figure and Essence of the 'New'

Recognition of China's architectural struggle for modernity in the 20th century has been a long time coming,[20] but the embrace of the 'new' has arrived with a dash and with intensity. This book, after all, is evidence of one such recognition. After almost a century's absence from Western scrutiny, China's new architecture is, all of sudden, 'here', with a demand to be discoursed. As with any book of architectural works and projects, the selection of works in this book is both conscious and circumstantial. It is, in other words, neither complete nor exclusive, but it does, nonetheless present a few common threads, which will, I hope, assist readers to find a path through the 'weeds' in order to search for the 'flowers' in China's emerging architecture. And, hopefully these 'flowers' will duly bear 'fruit'. As the individual projects will be given due care in the following pages, my aim here is to provide a guide for such navigation.

In spite of the sheer size and quantity of the urban projects, the glittering of China's new architecture may initially seem to be no different to that of the West. Many of the large-scale urban projects have been, and are being, built with state-of-the-art technology, and are clad with gleaming metal, glass and marble. There is, however, one distinctive feature of these new projects; many of them, be they designed by foreign architects or by local Chinese, are the result of a figurative concept, hence they look figuratively recognizable, although the figurative reading by the public can be amusingly different from the intention of the architect. Shanghai's 'Oriental Pearl', the city's monumental and highly conspicuous television tower, is often 'dubbed' as a 'chicken leg' by the locals. This sort of 'misreading' can lead to the frustration of the architect, as shown in the recent saga of the Shanghai World Financial Center, currently under construction in the same area as the 'Oriental Pearl'. The architects, Kohn Pedersen Fox, intended to reflect the Chinese cosmic model of 'square earth and round heaven', with the tower's square column intersected by two sweeping arcs, resulting in a slender crown punctuated by a large circle (page 10). The Shanghainese, knowing that Japanese money was behind the project, decided to see this figurative motif as two Japanese army swords holding a Japanese flag over Shanghai – a regrettable metaphor in light of 20th century history – and the construction was halted. The architect's response to this public rage was, once again, figurative: the circle is now intersected by a bridge, and is thus transformed into a Chinese 'moon gate'.[21]

A figurative concept, and its materialization in the design, has almost become a pre-requisite to win any large-scale project in China these days. To name a few more included in this book: Paul Andreu's National Grand Theater in Beijing has a large bubble 'heaven' hovering above the 'earth' of the theaters, which we might see as a

Figure 9: Beijing Capital International Airport
Beijing 2007 (estimated completion date)
Architect – Foster and Partners

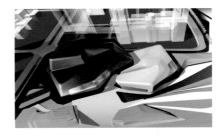

Figure 10: Guangzhou Opera House
Guangzhou 2005-
Architect – Zaha Hadid

Figure 11: Shanghai Opera House
Shanghai 1994-1998
Architect – Arte Jean-Marie Charpentier et Associés

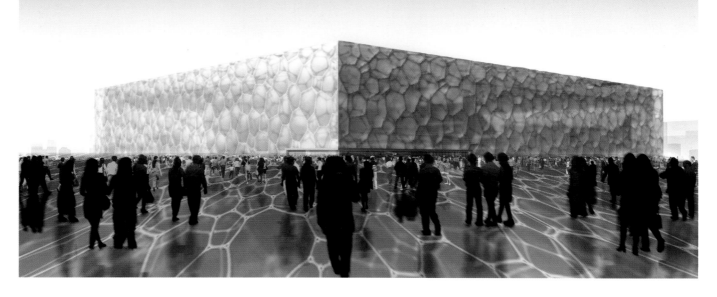

depiction of the Chinese cosmos (figure 8); another Chinese 'cosmos' is the Shanghai Opera House (1994-1998) by Arte Charpentier et Associés, which has a curved top and cubic square body (figure 11) ; the Beijing International Airport (under construction) by Foster and Partners, albeit sleek and high-tech, is (according to the architects) a flying 'dragon' (figure 9); and the Jinmao Tower (1997-1999) in Shanghai by SOM is a Chinese pagoda, so the architects argue, though it is clad with intricate metal frames and shining glass (page 9). Other figurative motifs are not overtly Chinese, but they do appear to have won the hearts of the Chinese: Zaha Hadid's Guangzhou Opera House (under construction) is comprised of 'pebble stones' washed smooth by the city's Pearl River (figure 10), and the Shanghai Pudong International Airport (1999) by Paul Andreu is a 'seagull' ready to spread its wings. Beijing's Olympic National Stadium (under construction) by Herzog and de Meuron, perhaps the most glamorous project so far conceived, is a gigantic 'bird's nest', and the 'Watercube' National Swimming Center, designed by PTW, China State Construction Engineering Corporation and Arup Group (figure 12), is a transparent crystal cell structure, although the architects have tried to argue that the square plan is Chinese.

The list can go on, with many more planned. I have wondered as to why a century's dilemma between tradition and modernity – which was materialized in architecture as a difficult choice between, or a combination of, a Chinese *yiangshi* (loosely translated as style) and a modern building type and its look – has been so rapidly dissolved, at least in architecture, since the turn of the new millennium. It is as if a collective hunger for representation has made architecture, which is perhaps not the most effective vehicle in this regard, almost a substitute for words.

Of course not all large-scale urban projects in China are the result of figurative fantasies: Foster and Partner's Jiushi Corporation Building (1995-2001) in Shanghai is, for example, a subdued high-rise towering among its aggressive neighbours, but it still addresses one of Norman Foster's universal concerns, which is to supply natural ventilation via atrium-like sky gardens (figure 13). Architecturally, I would like to see this idea as an attempt to internalize skyscrapers, within which life is so often segregated on a single floor plate, and sealed behind glass curtain walls. In Foster's towers, this desire to accommodate the inhabitants and their lives within the building, in addition to the views that a skyscraper offers, is on the one hand, basic (this is the least of the things a building should do!), but is indeed honourable on the other, given that many high-rise buildings are not 'internalized' as such. Jianwai SOHO (2000-) in Beijing, by Japanese architect Riken Yamamoto, is deliberately figureless, comprising a group of square-planned towers with flat roofs and grid façades, which, ironically, stand

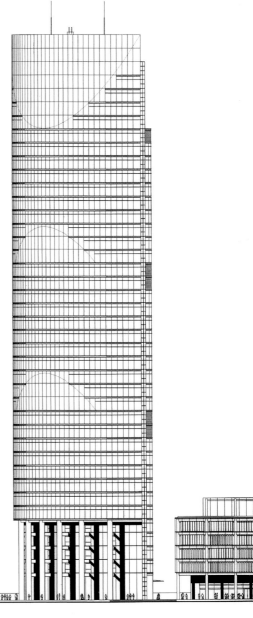

Jianwai SOHO
Beijing 2000-
Architect – Riken Yamamoto; Field Shop; C+A;
Mikan; Beijing New Era Architectural Design;
Beijing Dongfang Huatai Architecture and
Engineering

out among the continuing 'beauty contest' of high-rise towers in that city. But the intention here is not concerned with an 'abstract expression', rather it is an idea of a spatial configuration that separates cars from pedestrians, and gives pedestrians easy access to the buildings from the street in a context where private cars are increasingly regarded as the paramount symbol of modernity. If an analogy (not necessarily figurative) has to be used, it is that of a building type, and in Foster's case, we might say that a high-rise office building is like a garden. The metaphoric power of a figurative motif notwithstanding, the spatial configuration of building can be instrumental (to a degree) in structuring the lives of the inhabitants, which makes a building work!

In contrast, the group of young Chinese architects included in this book shy away from figurative approaches. Before I run a risk by generalizing some common characteristics that they may share, let me first examine their common 'rite of passage'. Typically, these architects began their architectural education in China after 1976, following the death of Chairman Mao and the fall of the 'Gang of Four'. Many of them went to Europe and North America to continue their education before, or immediately after, they finished their basic architectural studies in China. The education they received in China in the 1980s and for much of the 1990s carried a strong legacy of the Chinese Beaux-Arts, which had been well established between the 1920s and 1940s, when the first generation of American Beaux-Arts trained Chinese architects played significant roles in both practice and education. Due to a decade of 'suspension' in higher education during the Cultural Revolution from 1966 to 1976, surviving 'old generation' educators and architects, mostly in their 80s, returned to the universities to embrace the almost 'Renaissance' ambience of the later 1970s and early 1980s. Yang Tingbao, for example, remained as the spiritual leader of the Chinese architectural education until his death in 1982. When I started my architectural training in that same year at the highly regarded Nanjing Institute of Technology (the first architectural school established in China in the 1920s, now known as Southeast University) where Yang was based, the first studio assignment was to complete a Beaux-Arts ink rendering of a Chinese *yangshi*: a forceful composition of two building types, wherein the foreground stone tower is a Buddhist structure from 937-975 AD, and the background temple is a grand timber structure dated 1023-1032 AD (figure 14). Although some students elsewhere, Beijing's Tsinghua University for example, were allowed to render one of Vignola's orders, the Chinese *yangshi* was more or less preached as a cultural obligation.

Unlike the period between the 1920s and the 1940s, when China's architectural education was first established, the problem of style was a rather relaxed issue; a

Figure 14: Chinese Beaux-Arts rendering,
First Year Project by Xing Ruan, 1982.
Southeast University in Nanjing

Bamboo Wall House
Commune by the Great Wall, Shui Guan 2001
Architect - Kengo Kuma

Chinese *yangshi* was merely one of many styles that the students, and indeed the architects, could choose from, and they ranged from Renaissance, Spanish and French vernacular to Cubist and Modernist.[22] However, the students in 1980s China, the ambitious ones in particular, were impatient and hungry for modern and contemporary, hence the *yangshi* was often treated with disdain. Before any real sign of economic prosperity, and compounded by the political and ideological suppression of the 'new' and the 'Western' in the late 1980s (which peaked with the 1989 Tiananmen Square 'event'), many students chose to flee the country to search for the 'true modern' in the West. After more than a decade in the West – studying, teaching and doing paper architecture – on the eve of the Chinese economic boom, many made the timely return to grasp the unprecedented opportunities of design and getting projects built.

Among these 'returned' architects, Yung Ho Chang is one of the most prominent. After spending 15 years studying and teaching in the USA, he returned to Beijing in 1996 to establish his practice – Atelier FCJZ. His works have appeared in mainstream international journals, in 2000 he was the first Chinese architect to be invited to exhibit at the Venice Biennale (he also participated in the two subsequent exhibitions, and designed the Chinese Pavilion for the third), and he now receives frequent invitations to teach and to speak internationally. As a result of his success on the international stage and in the Western media, he is (at the time of writing this book) the designated Head of Architecture at MIT.[23] It seems Yung Ho Chang has, in just over two decades, drawn two full circles, which may well become a trend for his peers to follow.

Contrary to their initial urge to discover the true modernity in architecture when they left China for the West, Yung Ho Chang and many of his peers returned to China with a self-imposed mission: to create a contemporary – and culturally – Chinese architecture. This should not come as a surprise, but it is nonetheless intriguing when compared with the first generation of Chinese architects who trained in the West. Those who studied in America, Europe and Japan in the early part of the 20th century, searched for universal virtues in architecture under a Beaux-Arts education, and were hence encouraged to identify affinities between China and the West. When they returned to China in the first half of the 20th century, cultural and place identities were not the paramount problems facing them. But to the surprise of the new generation of young Chinese architects who landed in the 'post-modern' West of the 1980s, 'ethnicity' and 'diversity' were the buzzwords, from highbrow intellectual circles to pop culture. They were quick to realize that they were under pressure for being Chinese, and a cultural or place identity was an effective ticket to international recognition. *Fengshui*, for example, became one of the most popular research topics for

Tiantai Museum
Tiantai, Zhejiang Province 1999-2003
Architect - Wang Lu

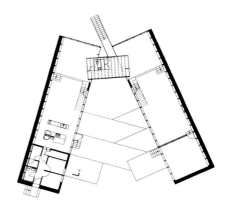

Figure 13: Split House, Commune by the Great Wall, Shui Guan 2001 - Yung Ho Chang, Atelier FCJZ.

Airport House
Commune by the Great Wall, Shui Guan 2001
Architect – Chien Hsueh-Yi

Chinese students in Western universities, and *Yin* and *Yang* frequently appeared in the entries of international idea competitions from these young architects. Some of Yung Ho Chang's competition winning schemes – such as his first prize in the 1986 Shinkenchiku Residential Design Competition – were subtly coated with Chinese concepts of rooms and space.

In his early experimental and built projects in China, Yung Ho Chang tried figurative motifs, such as bamboos for city planning, and bicycle wheels for bookstores. But one enduring theme in his work is a non-figurative building type – the courtyard. For Yung Ho Chang, a courtyard could confine a Chinese ambience, or a landscape ideal. At the Morningside Center of Mathematics (1998) in Beijing, Yung Ho Chang created a 'micro-city' by inserting what he called "squeezed" Chinese courtyards into a multi-storey building. In the Split House at the Commune by the Great Wall (2001), a courtyard created by literally 'splitting' the rammed earthed building, serves to 'contain' the landscape (figure 13).

The courtyard, though non-figurative, is a powerful configuration that encourages gregariousness, and is seen by like-minded Chinese architects as the essence of Chinese architecture, something that can be re-fabricated in the modern and the contemporary. Wang Lu's use of courtyards in the Tiantai Museum (1999-2003) has not only has created an intimate domestic scale, but also ensures that the museum offers alternatives for the visitor, in order to break away from a sequential circulation. Other architects from the same generation, such as Wang Shu and Liu Jiakun, never studied in the West, but did good modernist 'homework' in China. Wang Shu's Wenzheng College Library (2001), although only crudely realized in the plan, has attempted to recreate the density and intimacy of the alleyways of southern Chinese cities. Liu Jiakun, resisting the temptation of a transparent and free plan, has tried to choreograph a Zen plot with the twists and turns of bridges and walls within the courtyard of the studio residence (1995-1996) for sculptor He Douling (figures 14 and 15).

Not everyone in this new group is overtly concerned with a Chinese-ness in their architectural works, and some of them have also attracted international limelight. Ma Qinyun, like Rem Koolhaas, is interested in the 'ecstasy' of the speed of Chinese urbanization and its mammoth scale. The international interest in their works is, I suppose, due to a fascination with their rapid achievement of modern and contemporary. But for most of these younger architects, the real meaning of international acknowledgment is in the appraisal of their original intentions. When twelve Asian architects were selected to design the villas in the Commune by the Great Wall, they were prejudged according to their 'contemporariness' and by their

Figure 14: He Douling Studio, Chengdu
1995-1996 – Liu Jiakun

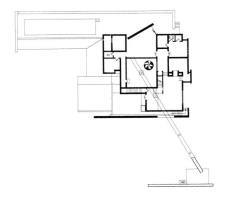

Figure 15: He Douling Studio, Chengdu
1995-1996 – Liu Jiakun – first floor plan.

Luyeyuan Stone Sculpture Museum
Chengdu 2001-2002
Architect – Liu Jiakun

individual methods of using 'traditional' materials. When the entire project received the award for the 'Promotion of Architectural Art' at the 2002 Venice Biennale, it was praised by curator Deyan Sudjic as a 'combination of aesthetic ambition and the reinforcement of Asian identity through architectural innovation'. If the aversion to a figurative motif is to give way to the instrumental capacity of a spatial configuration, hence the power of an idea, my sense is that, at some point, these architects will demand to be recognized not only circumstantially as Chinese architects, but also universally as good architects.

The Good

It would be frivolous to argue that Yung Ho Chang's rammed earth construction and courtyard 'vagaries' are some sort of Chinese specificity; surely they are quite universal across space and time. The Chinese cosmic model of square earth and round heaven, needless to say, no longer holds any real validity to govern the worldview of a modern citizen. Even the cosmic model itself, a stratified universe, was once a shared diagram among many pre-modern peoples. Regardless of its 'looks', the new architecture, Chinese or not, is, and inevitably will be, kitsch. The real test, however, lies in the power of the idea, and of more importance, the 'goodness' of an idea that reflects fundamental human conditions.

While we are enjoying the blossom of 'a hundred flowers' in China's emerging new architecture, and indeed embracing the vitality of the 'new', we should be reminded that the Good, like the Bad, is also a universal validity. Iris Murdoch has this un-compromised view of bad art: '...there is nothing mysterious about the forms of bad art since they are recognizable and familiar rat-runs of selfish day-dream.'[24] The consequences of bad architecture, which is at the scale of splendor, are far more consequential and instrumental than any other form of art. The austere 'look' of 20th century modern architecture does not necessarily lead to the Good; conversely, the kitsch may embody a universal virtue.

At the closing ceremony of the 2004 Athens Olympic Games, the Chinese staged a show to give the world a tantalising glimpse of what might be expected at the 2008 Beijing Olympic Games: young girls, each with a *pipa* (a Chinese string instrument) in their hands and clad in Chinese costumes, sang and danced to the cheeky Chinese folk tune 'Jasmine Flower', but they did so in tightly-fitting mini skirts... kitsch it may have been, but the air was filled with sweetness. Who does not admire the 'free beauty' of a flower, as Immanuel Kant once asked?

*Left: 'Watercube' National
Swimming Center
Beijing 2007
(estimated completion date)
Architect – PTW Architects;
China State Construction Engineering
Corporation; Arup Group*

*Right: Olympic National Stadium
Beijing 2008
(estimated completion date)
Architect – Herzog and de Meuron;
Arup Group*

Footnotes

1 Chuihua Judy Chung, and others, eds., *Great Leap Forward: Harvard Design School Project on the City* (Cambridge, Mass., 2001).

2 More books of this kind seem to pop up now and then. Architectural writer Neil Leach, for example, wrote a book entitled *China* in a short period of six weeks. The theme, not surprisingly, is based on the enormity and speed of China's urbanization. Neil Leach, *China* (Hong Kong, 2004).

3 "On the Correct Handling of Contradictions Among the People" in *Quotations from Chairman Mao Tse-tung* (Zedong) (1st pocket ed., Chinese version, 1957, Peking [Beijing]), 49-50. English translation in Quotations from Chairman Mao Tse-tung (Zedong), (Peking [Beijing] 1966), 302-303. Legend has it that the Chinese literary giant Qian Zhongshu was appointed to the English translator-in-chief for Mao's works, but the translators were anonymous in this publication.

4 Iris Murdoch, *The Sovereignty of Good* (London and New York, 1970).

5 Yi-Fu Tuan, *Morality and Imagination* (Wisconsin, 1989), 97.

6 Author's recollection of Kenneth Frampton's keynote address at the Beijing UIA Congress in 1999. In his address, Frampton reflects upon 'other' modern architecture that was not included in his book, *Modern Architecture: A Critical History* (London, 1985).

7 See, for example, Xing Ruan "Paradox of the Hidden Figure", in *Yung Ho Chang: Atelier Feichang Jianzhu- A Chinese Practice* (Paris and Hong Kong, 2003), 25-36.

8 Liang Sicheng, known as Liang Ssu-ch'eng in the West, is the son of the famous late-Qing reformer Liang Qichao. Liang Sicheng is best known for his scholarly work in documenting historical Chinese architecture with Western conventions. In the 1930s, Liang Sicheng, together with his wife Lin Whei-yin and others, such as Liu Dunzheng, studied and recorded some significant remaining pieces of pre-modern Chinese architecture. This was the first time that Chinese architecture was recorded and drawn in scale using Western conventions. Early English publications of his research, such as "Open Spandrel Bridges of Ancient China," in *Pencil Points*, part 1, 19 (1938): 25-32 and part 2, 19 (1938): 155-160, appeared in the 1930s. As a result of these publications, Liang received invitations from Yale University and Princeton University to teach, as well as an invitation to speak at an international conference in 1946 and 1947. Some of his immaculate drawings of traditional Chinese architecture were accompanied with English annotations for Western readership, and were finally published by the MIT Press in 1984, long after Liang's death. See Ssu-ch'eng Liang, *A Pictorial History of Chinese Architecture: A Study of the Development of Its Structural System* (Cambridge,

Mass., 1984), and Wilma Fairbank, *Liang and Lin: Partners in Exploring China's Architectural Past* (Philadelphia, 1994). Also see Ann L. Strong and George E. Thomas, eds., *The Book of the School: 100 Years* (Philadelphia, 1990), 88.

9 See Strong and Thomas, *The Book of the School*, 31 (n. 8). However, to what extent 20th century Chinese architecture was shaped by these Penn-trained architects is not elaborated in *The Book of the School*. New scholarship on these architects and early 20th-century Chinese architecture are beginning to emerge in the English language. See, for example, Xing Ruan, "Accidental Affinities: American Beaux-Arts in Twentieth-century Chinese Architectural Education and Practice," in JSAH 61 (2002): 30-47; and Peter Rowe and Seng Kuan, *Architectural Encounters with Essence and Form in Modern China* (Cambridge, Mass., 2002).

10 See Ruan, (n. 9); essay 'Accidental Affinities'. Described as 'the most distinguished student', Yang Tingbao is, however, not listed among the ninety-nine biographies of the eminent alumni included in *The Book of the School* (see n. 9). Indeed, only Liang Sicheng is selected from the group of Chinese students. A few other Chinese students are mentioned, although only in the context of Liang's biography; they include Yang Tingbao, Lin Whei-yin and Chen Zhi. Yang Tingbao, B.Arch. 1924, M.Arch. 1925, known as T'ing-pao Yang at Penn winning three major awards from the Beaux-Arts Institute of Design: the Municipal Art Prize, the Emerson Prize and the Warren Prize. He also won the Samuel Huckel Jr. Prize, 1922-23, and the Sigma Xi, honorary fraternity for scientific achievement. Lin Whei-yin, known as Phyllis Lin at Penn, graduated in 1927 and later became Liang's wife and partner. As a female student, Lin was not allowed to enrol in the architecture programme; she received her degree in Fine Arts. Chen Zhi, known as Benjamin C. Chen at Penn, B.Arch/M.Arch, 1927, was the winner of the Cope Memorial Award for his redesign of the northwest corner of City Hall.

11 Yang Tingbao, *Yang Tingbao jianzhu sheji zuoping ji* (Yang Tingbao, architectural works and projects) (Beijing, 1983).

12 In addition to the numerous modern and contemporary superstar Japanese architects, some Indian architects, such as Charles Correa and Balkrishna Doshi, are included in the centre of contemporary architectural discourse.

13 Frampton, *Modern Architecture*, (see n. 6)

14 Arthur Danto believes that this is the second wave of Japanese influence on modern Western art; essentially, which seemed to have happened in visual arts before it reached architecture, both in Japan and in the West. See 'Munakata in New York: A Memory of the 1950s' in *Philosophizing Art*, (Berkeley and Los Angeles, 1999) 164-184.

15 See, for example, John Musgrove, ed., *Sir Banister*

Fletcher's A History of Architecture (London, 1987). In this nineteenth edition, the famous "Tree of Architecture," in which pre-modern Chinese architecture appeared in the early stage as a tree branch and disappeared in the progress of architectural history is already edited out. Instead, the cover image is the interior of the Gate of Nijo Castle in Kyoto.

16 Frampton, *Modern Architecture* (see n. 6).

17 This is also reflected in the writings by Chinese scholars for Western audiences; appearing to be a legacy of Liang's. Professor Liu Guanghua (known as Laurence Liu in the West), a Nanjing School graduate in the 1940s, after more than thirty years teaching and practicing architecture in modern China, went to the US in the 1980s to teach and write about pre-modern Chinese architecture. His monumental book, *Chinese Architecture* (New York, 1989), ironically, had no room for modern and contemporary Chinese architecture.

18 Before the 1999 UIA Congress in Beijing, Kenneth Frampton was appointed as chief editor for a ten-volume *World Architecture 1900-2000: A Critical Mosaic*; which was to be published by the China Architecture and Building Press. This multi-volume book series has recorded 20th century architecture on a global scale. In the introduction, Frampton says that there are two factors that bring together such a compendium: "...first an obligation to bring China into the world debate on the future of architecture and second, a concomitant need to reactivate China's own architectural culture, after a century of rather varied and uncertain eclecticism, beginning with the arrival of foreign architects in Shanghai soon after the turn of the century" (Beijing and New York, 2000), XIV.

19 Edward Said, *The World, the Text, and the Critic* (Cambridge, Mass., 1983), 227.

20 See Ruan, 'Accidental Affinities', and Rowe and Kuan, *Architectural Encounters*, (both appear in n. 9).

21 Joseph Rykwert has made similar remarks in his *The Seduction of Place: The History and Future of the City* (New York, 2002) 221-222.

22 For a detailed discussion of early Chinese education and American Beaux-Arts, see Ruan, "Accidental Affinities" (n. 9).

23 For a full discussion of Yung Ho Chang's works, see Ruan, "Paradox" (n. 7).

24 Murdoch, *Sovereignty of Good*, 84 (n. 4).

Beijing Capital
International Airport

Beijing 2007 (estimated completion date)

Architect Foster and Partners

Norman Foster obviously got the *fengshui* right for the Hong Kong and Shanghai Bank (Hong Kong, 1985) - he hired a *fengshui* master to advise him about the angle of the escalator linking the street to the first level – as well as the symbolic significance of the Hong Kong International Airport, which was completed for the 1997 Hong Kong handover and foreshadowed his fortune in China. The structural elegance and circulation clarity of the Hong Kong airport is indeed state-of-the-art, and its spectacular foreshore site has made departure and arrival glamorous, even for an economy class traveler.

The site of the new Beijing International Airport is no match for that of Hong Kong, so the architects have to rely on artificially created splendor: the configuration is that of two Ys joined together, envisaged by the architects as two Chinese ideograms for 'human' when viewed from the air. Since the site is so flat and featureless, the illuminated night images sing exclusive praises to the occupation of the earth by human beings… a *topophilia*, as geographer Yi-fu Tuan might call it! The configuration conveniently follows the circulation logic of an airport; one Y receives arriving cars and trains, while the other one greets the landing planes. And it is no surprise that the architects have given the gigantic curving roof a Chinese anthropomorphic connotation, a 'flying dragon', and the dense south east facing sky-windows do appear like scales when viewed from the ground. Despite its status as a national totem, not every Chinese thinks the dragon a particularly elegant animal, although it appears that this sleek Foster 'dragon' will win the hearts of many when completed.

This project will cost 2 billion US dollars, and is planned to be complete in 2007 for the 2008 Beijing Olympics. Like many Foster buildings, the terminal will be assembled on site with prefabricated components, and promises to be one of the world's most technically advanced and sustainable buildings. As the city of Beijing is eager to announce its global city status, nothing could be more propitious than a Foster airport for the 2008 Olympic Games.

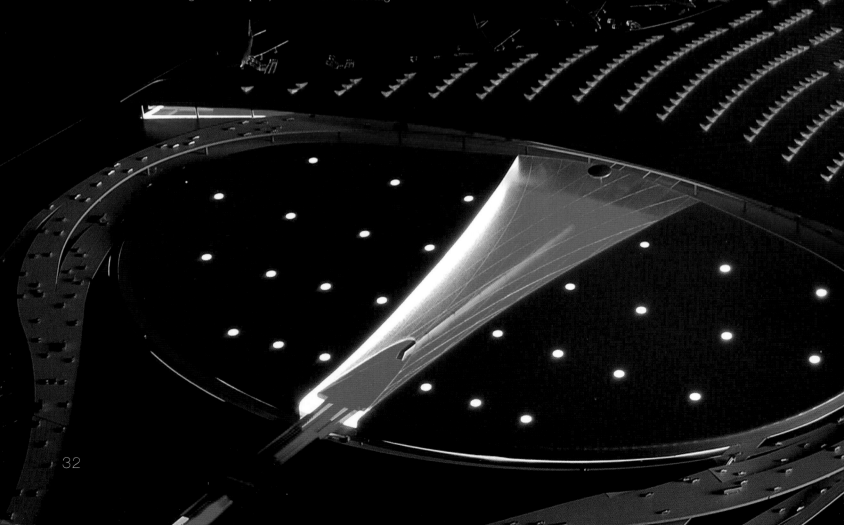

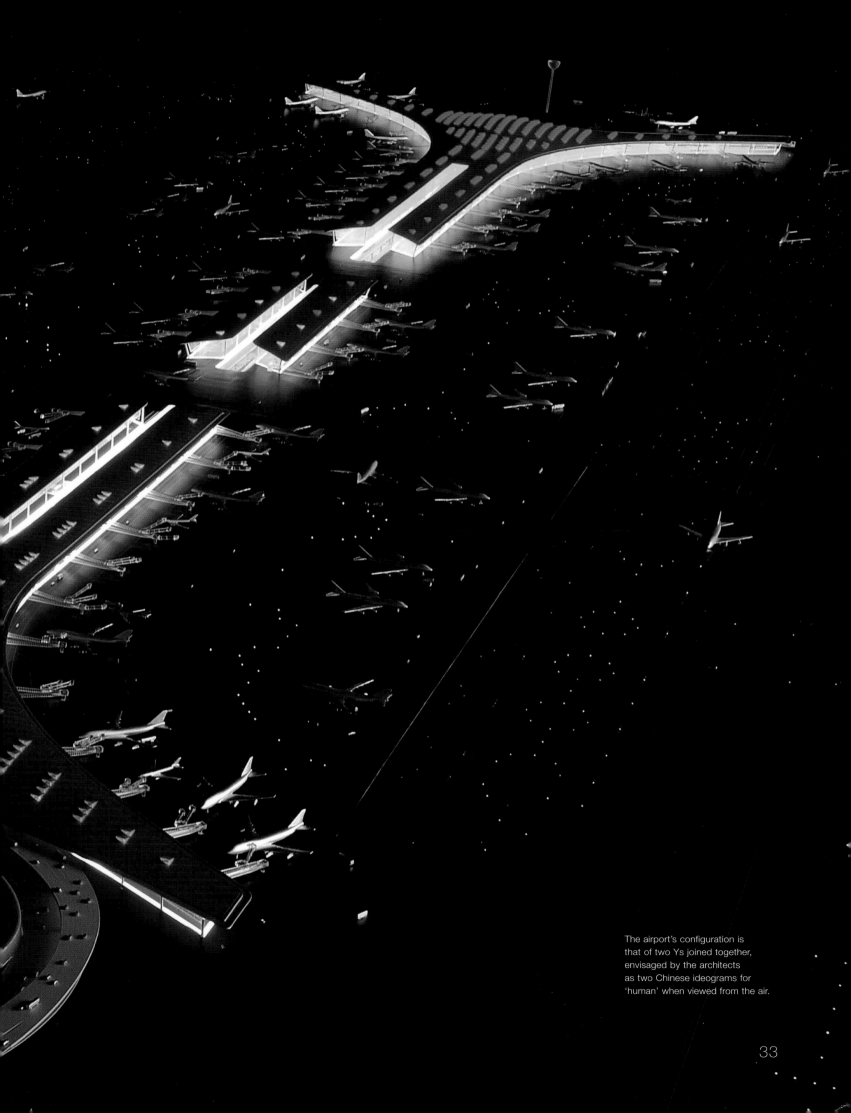

The airport's configuration is that of two Ys joined together, envisaged by the architects as two Chinese ideograms for 'human' when viewed from the air.

33

Right: The plan clearly shows the logic of the airport's circulation, with one Y receiving car and train passengers, while the other embraces arriving planes.

Below: The gigantic curving roof has been given the anthropomorphic connotation of a 'flying dragon'.

Below right: The south east facing sky-windows appear as 'dragon's scales'.

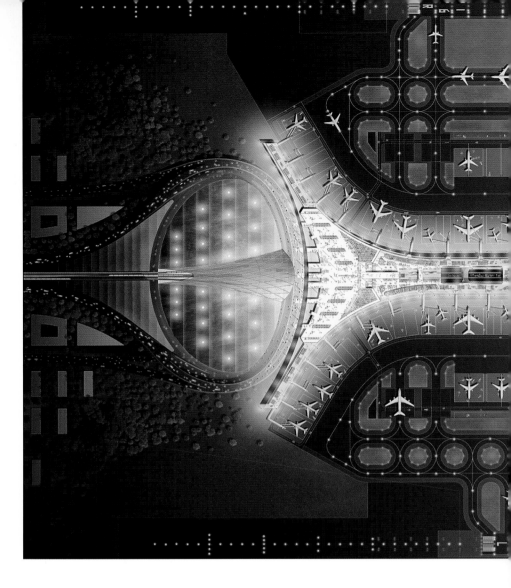

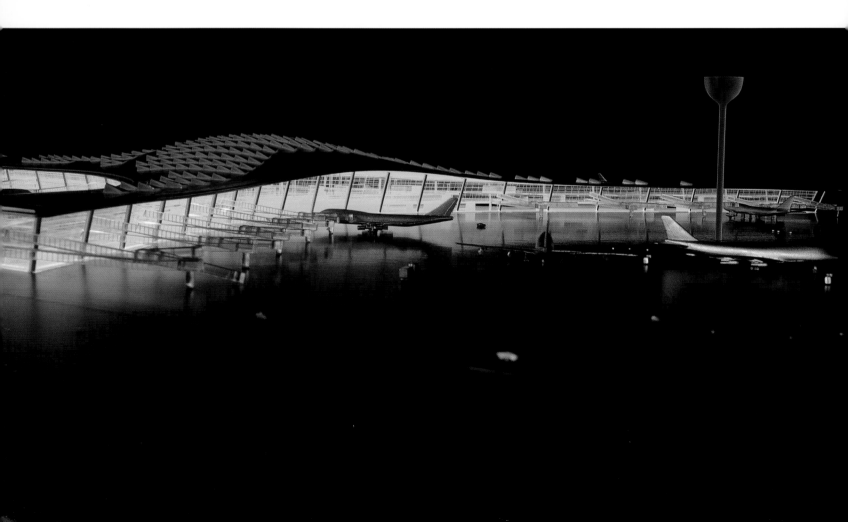

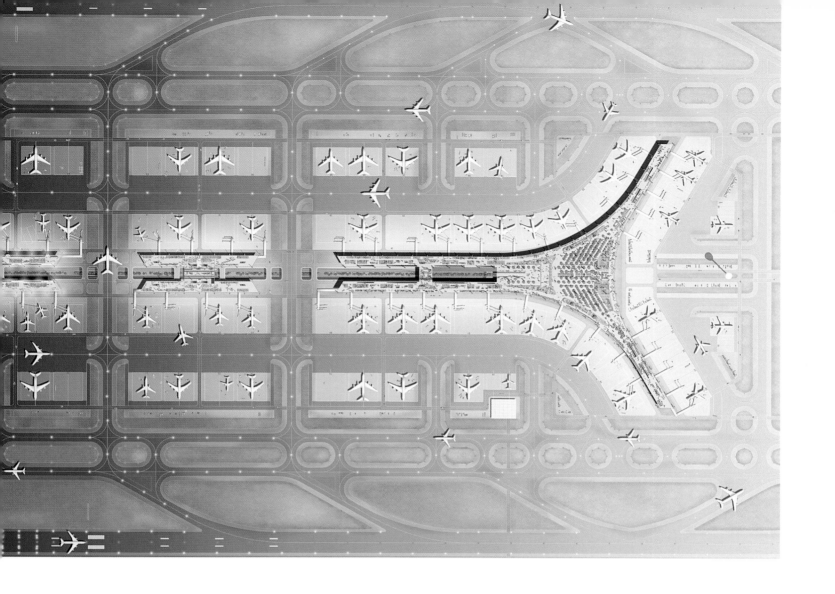

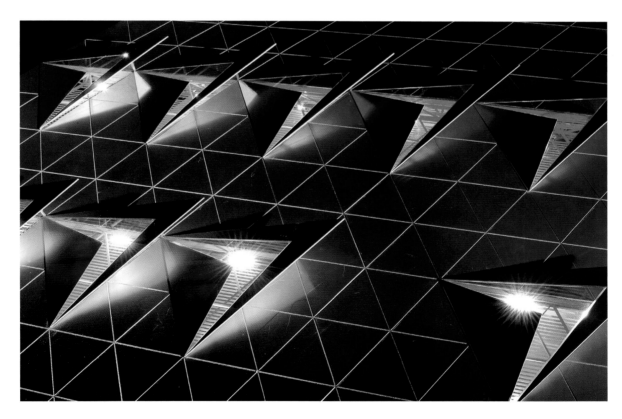

BEIJING CAPITAL INTERNATIONAL AIRPORT

35

Jianwai SOHO

Beijing   2000-

Architect Riken Yamamoto; Field Shop; C+A; Mikan; Beijing New Era Architectural
Design; Beijing Dongfang Huatai Architecture and Engineering

Jianwai SOHO, 2 miles east of Tiananmen Square, is a new living, working and shopping complex at the 'high end' of the market. It includes high-rise apartment towers (many of which combine small offices with living areas), a three-storey retail podium, office space and underground parking. The entire Jianwai SOHO complex will have a 'mega' 700,000 square meters of floor space when complete. The first stage, conceptualized and master planned by the Beijing-born Japanese architect Riken Yamamoto, was finished in late 2003 and has already become a much desired address for cosmopolitan urban living in China, attracting high-earning young professionals and their kindred spirits to form a community. Pan Shiyi, the project's celebrity developer, had already made his name with the much-publicized Commune by the Great Wall, west of Beijing.

Most of the high-rise towers are square in plan, with a nearly square white-gridded façade, and all have flat roofs, in stark contrast to the current Beijing 'architectural gymnastics', where new high-rise buildings typically have different shapes and tops. Jianwai SOHO appears sober, but with luxury touches… the façade grid, for example, is clad with white marble. Dubbed as 'abstract architectural expression' by some architectural critics and commentators, this sobriety is a conscious decision by the architect. But the underlying design idea is more radical than the look of the buildings, as the plan grid is slanted 25 degrees

Left and above: Jianwai SOHO appears sober, but with luxury touches... the nearly square gridded façade is clad with white marble.

from Beijing's imperial cardinal grid. This aims to ensure that all high-rise towers receive sufficient sunlight, to avoid visual intrusions from each other, and to align the buildings with the nearby Tonghui River, which is not orthogonal to the city grid of Beijing. This break from Beijing's grid is indeed rare! Perhaps even more radical is Yamamoto's decision to separate cars from pedestrians: cars are parked on the two underground parking levels, so that pedestrians have unimpeded access to the shopping and office areas from the street. This may seem quite a reasonable approach elsewhere, but should be considered bold in China, for private cars are increasingly worshipped as a symbol of modern life. Various large openings are punched through the floors to the lower levels to create sky-lit gardens, which bring light to the car parks. Apartment plans are typically a grouping of enclosed rooms with open plan living, dining and home office spaces. Some kitchens are part of the open plan, but some are enclosed in deference to the smoking stir-fry Chinese cooking.

I can see Yamamoto's decision to treat cars with less respect than humans as honorable, but what does pedestrian access mean to Chinese urban life? Joseph Rykwert has observed that the wide bases of high-rise buildings in early 20th century New York were accessible to pedestrians... it was a time when the American dream was still 'dreamed' by everyone in the street. But the last two decades of 'pencil point' skyscrapers rise abruptly from their bases, and their elegant foyers are heavily guarded! The message, Rykwert says, is that American dreams are now reserved only for those who have "enough income to sleep on." When Jianwai SOHO was published in the Japanese JA magazine, the sleek interior with pointy modern furniture (a Mies van der Rohe glass-top coffee table, for example) was juxtaposed with a sloppily dressed maid, presumably from the countryside, who is mopping the shining floor. One wonders whether this new urban environment enshrines her dream, if not an American one.

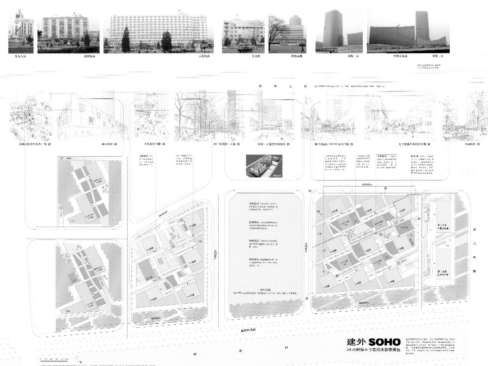

Above left: The two towers on the eastern edge of the site have a rectangular footprint.

Above: The architect decided to separate cars from pedestrians, so that pedestrians may have unimpeded access to the shopping and office areas. Cars are parked underground.

Above and right: The Jianwai SOHO complex comprises high-rise apartment towers, three-storey retail podiums, office space and underground parking. With the urban professional in mind, many of the apartments combine small offices with the living areas.

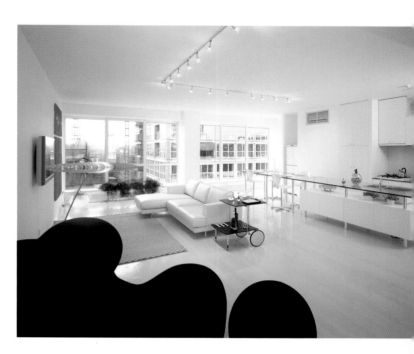

National Grand Theater

Beijing 2006 (estimated completion date)

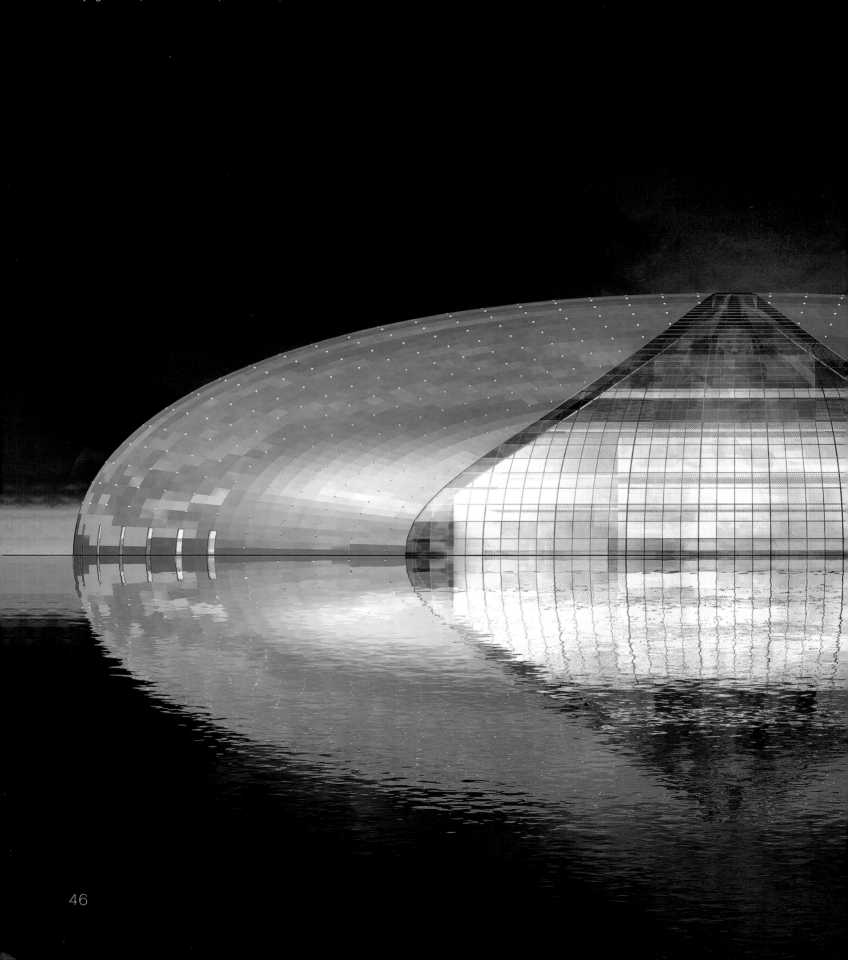

French architect Paul Andreu won the National Grand Theater international competition ahead of a galaxy of international star architects, including Arata Isozaki and Hans Hollein. Though it was never an issue for the Chinese to engage with Andreu to design an opera house - he is generally known as an airport architect and his Shanghai Pudong International Airport is included elsewhere in this book - opinions have, nonetheless, been polarized in terms of the design.

The theater is located immediately to the west of the Great Hall of the People on Changan Avenue, the symbolic spine of Beijing running from east to west across the city's south-north imperial axis of Tiananmen Square and the formal imperial palace of the Forbidden City. The design comprises a gigantic glass sphere hovering above the water in a large pond, and this sphere has an east-to-west span of 213 meters, with a 144 meter north-to-south span, and the height is 46 meters, which is exactly the same height as the Great Hall of People. No doubt the architect would have used this to counter criticism that his futurist 'blob' does not fit the neo-Classical context, but this, more than anything, is where opinion is divided.

A feature of the design is its entry tunnel under the artificial lake, as the complex is sunken below ground level. This tunnel, according to the architect, allows preparation with space and time for entering the theater. The curved earthy-red masonry wall - the only reminder of the Forbidden City across the road - naturally leads to the underwater tunnel. Surely it will be a fascinating experience to go through the glazed tunnel as if a fish swimming in the lake, which, in my frivolous imagination, would serve as a purifying ritual for people entering from a delirious consumer's world to acquire some culture. Not so frivolous is a figurative nickname for the titanium-clad sphere from the Chinese: the 'eggshell'. This always happens to an iconic building, and I doubt it would be called something else if it were built elsewhere. Three separate buildings - the central opera house, the concert hall and the theater - are covered by the 'eggshell', and the space between

Above: Entry to the theater from Changan Avenue is through a curved red wall to an underwater tunnel.

Right: The silver titanium shell is divided by a glass façade in the shape of a water droplet, which curves up from a 100 meter base on the north and south to form a narrow sliver at roof level.

the shell and these buildings naturally becomes the concourse. In the concourse, amenities and viewing platforms on various levels face Changan Avenue through a large glass surface in the shape of a water drop, which symmetrically splits the titanium-clad shell into two parts. In most opera houses, the space between the shell and the theater is unknown... the Sydney Opera House is one example in which the shell provides the external image, while the internal envelope serves the performance and acoustics; the space between is hidden. One advantage of a shell covering separate buildings is the legibility of each building within the 'complex'. In sharp contrast to the external silver titanium surface, the entire interior layer of the shell is clad with mahogany timber stripes, which give an over-arching warm tone to this small universe. Although an egg has a universal symbolic connotation of fertility (and it is no exception for the Chinese), Wolfram Eberhard reminds us that one school of antique Chinese astronomy actually believes that the cosmos is egg-shaped: the earth is inside the shell, completely covered by it, and resting like a yolk on the fluid white, which is incubated by the heaven. One is tempted to speculate that Andreu won this competition because his eggshell, subconsciously, touches a Chinese nerve. Evidence has it that opera houses will soon mushroom in other Chinese capital cities, and they may even be seen in wealthy country towns. It is hard to image that Italian operas will flourish all over China, but there is no doubt that various shapes of 'cosmos' will be built.

Left: The interior spaces of the complex have been designed with an 'open, popular character' in mind. The opera house is covered with a gilt metal mesh, and the concourse areas comprise shopping precincts, restaurants and waiting lounges on many levels.

Above: A cross-section through the theater complex from the west, with the Great Hall of the People in the background. The height of the National Grand Theater is the same – 46 meters – as the Great Hall of the People.

Below: The glistening 'eggshell' emerges from a newly created lake... its elliptical shape contrasting with the neo-Classical context of Tiananmen Square. According to the architect, the design intended "to create a building that shows respect for the buildings around it."

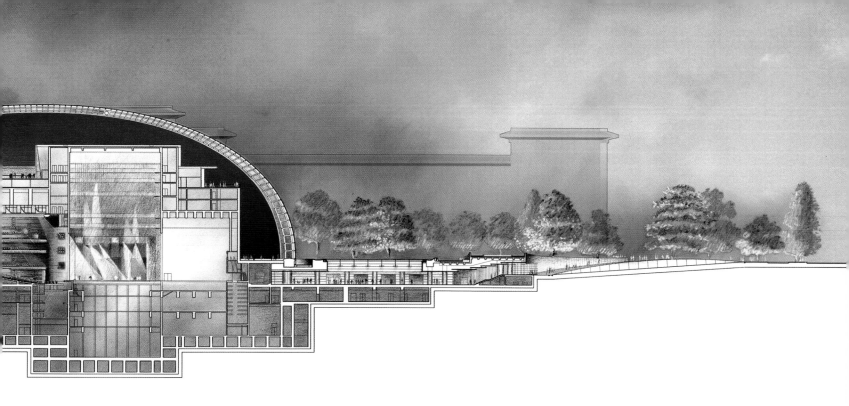

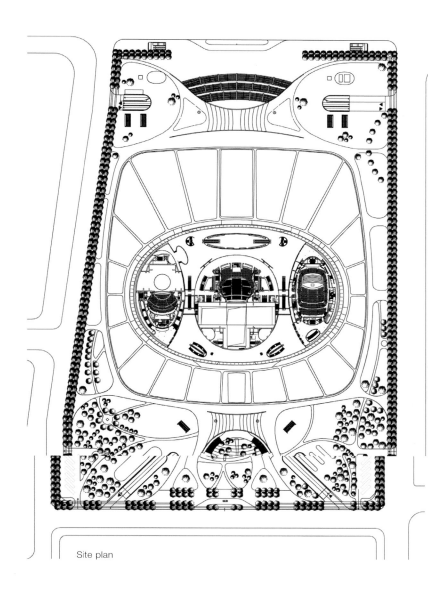

Site plan

National Institute
of Accountancy

Beijing 2003

Architect Qi Xin

A national training retreat for charted accountants, the institute is located near the Beijing International Airport and is bound by two freeways; it occupies an open site of 133,400 square meters with 70,000 square meters of inhabitable floor area. Given its 18-meter height limit, as well as its location, it is truly a suburban campus, but it is unclear though, why accountants in China should be trained in a secluded environment out in the suburbs. Bicycles are seen in the artistic impressions of the project, but I cannot imagine the poor accountants riding their bicycles from downtown Beijing, many miles from this location. They must have private cars...

As the road grid is 45 degrees to the orthogonal cardinal grid, which is paramount to building orientation in China, a north-south axis has been introduced to the master plan, with an oval shape in order to soften its conflict with the neighboring freeway grid. Further to the thrust of the master plan, the main teaching building is also an oval-shaped 'liner' building with the two façades facing south and north. It may make some sense that this spaceship-like main building should be wrapped with glass from 'head to toe' to look high-tech and futuristic, but an inner layer of plywood is required to ensure that the lecture theaters are black boxes. One advantage is that the shapes of lecture theaters are visually recognizable from the outside! The same clean-cut crisp glass façade has been applied to other public buildings, such as the curved student center and the library, and the large surrounding open space is enhanced by well-designed landscaping. It must be said that this level of integrity between building design and open space is exemplary in China. The adjacent dormitories are built from heavy masonry, and designed with urban scale internal courts, creating an ensemble which appears like a peculiar marriage between a neo-Classical French court and a Jean Nouvel dematerialization.

The triple-layer glass façade is intricate, and technically advanced in terms of energy performance in ventilation and thermal control. As shoddy workmanship is still a big issue in China, the architects have indicated a rare competence in the use of technology, and in achieving a quality building finish. But the question of why a large area of glazing is used in the first place should be asked. A much larger issue should provoke an overdue debate about this tendency of suburbanizing institutions. Is this what the Chinese need from the 20th century West? Leaving the quality of life aside, what is the global energy implication of Chinese suburbanization? Architects surely should assume the responsibility in initiating, and indeed participating in this debate.

Right: The main teaching building viewed from the east.

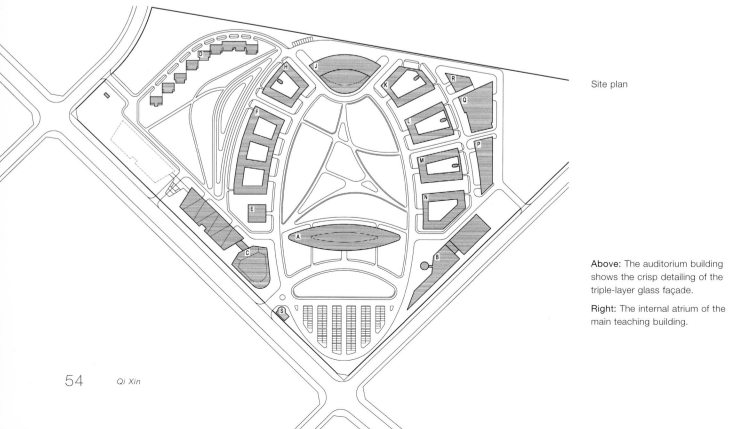

Site plan

Above: The auditorium building shows the crisp detailing of the triple-layer glass façade.

Right: The internal atrium of the main teaching building.

Teaching building
plan

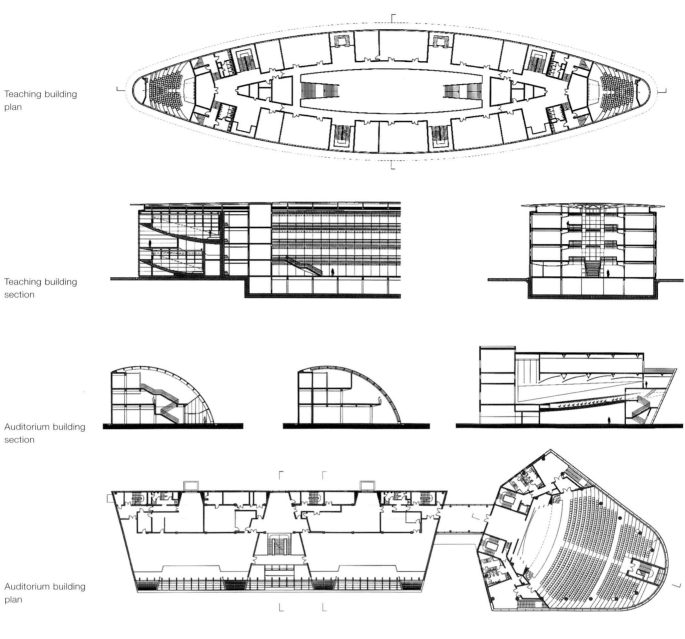

Teaching building
section

Auditorium building
section

Auditorium building
plan

China Central Television (CCTV) Headquarters

Beijing 2008 (estimated completion date)

Architect Rem Koolhaas and OMA

Rem Koolhaas and the CCTV headquarters would appear to be a perfect fit between the architect and the building. From his claim of Asian 'generic cities', to his China Pearl River Delta research project, and to his recent Harvard project on shopping, Koolhaas has proved to be an architect who understands the power of the media, and knows how to use it in effective ways. His books are bestsellers, and he is doing exceedingly well in China. It does seem to make sense that the competition for a landmark building of media conglomerate CCTV should be won by Koolhaas and his Office for Metropolitan Architecture. It also makes sense that the competition jurors included architect Arata Isozaki and critic Charles Jencks, who are forever searching for 'new paradigms' in architecture. All the 'star signs' suggest that this building must define something 'new'.

This complex is located on a 10-hectare site in Beijing's newly defined CBD, a notion, like 'suburbia', unheard of in China just a few years ago. It is also among the first of 300 new towers to be built in this new CBD. Of a total floor area of 553,000 square meters, 405,000 square meters comprise the CCTV headquarters

tower, and the remaining 116,000 square meters make up the Television Cultural Centre (TVCC). The CCTV tower includes administration, news, broadcasting, studios and program production – the entire process of TV making is designed as a sequence of interconnected activities. The TVCC includes a hotel, a visitor's center, a large public theater and exhibition spaces.

The CCTV tower, which looks more futuristic than the TVCC, does possess several new features previously unseen in conventional towers. This 230-meter tall tower is actually a twin-tower, connected both on the ground and at the top as a twisted loop. The irregular grid on the building surface represents, according to the architect, the forces travelling throughout the structure. This design idea would though, be impossibly legible for someone on the street, and it also raises the question of why a Chinese media conglomerate would want to express the structural forces of its building. The juxtaposition of the fully glazed, hence transparent, building surface with an irregular grid would seem to symbolically reveal the hidden institutional power struggle in a large state-owned organization. It is safe to assume that the Chinese authorities do not interpret this symbolism as a general cry for independent journalism, otherwise the project would not have received the green light. The TVCC is marked with a hotel tower and a cultural complex podium; only the matching shapes with the CCTV tower suggest they belong to the same 'newness'.

The 'newness' of this Koolhaas building has triggered debates. The questions raised by Chinese architects range from the structural integrity of its irregular shape to the astronomical cost of the project, and to the apparent lack of decorum shown to Beijing's historical context. Given that almost all the major public projects in China are now won by celebrity foreign architects (which this book clearly shows), some Chinese architects believe that China has become an experimental laboratory for foreign architects, and an 'architectural colonization' is now taking place. All this aside, one more question should have been asked at the outset: when the 'newness' of the CCTV building becomes worn and dated, how will one reconcile such an 'historical style' with the intrinsic nature of the media, which is solely concerned with 'newness'?

Above and left: The 230 meter tall CCTV tower is actually a twin tower, connected both on the ground and at the top as a twisted loop. According to the architect, the irregular grid on the building's façades "is an expression of the forces travelling throughout its structure."

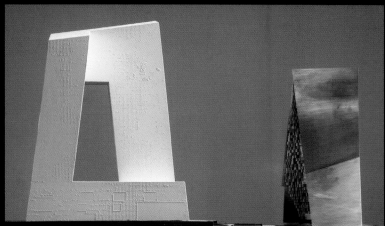

Top left: The CCTV and the TVCC towers seen in the context of Beijing's new CBD.

Left: The fully glazed, hence transparent, building surface is juxtaposed with an irregular grid.

Above: Models of the project show the patterns of the irregular grid of the facades.

798 New
Art District

Da Shanzi, Beijing 2002-

The 798 New Art District, in the Beijing suburb of Da Shanzi, has evolved in three years to become a 'globally hip' destination comprised of artist's studios, art galleries and dealers, cafés, restaurants and bookstores. The vibrant complex is contained within a factory designed by East German architects in the 1950s, and never in their wildest dreams would those architects have envisaged such a scene in their clean-cut functionally driven design. The factory, typical of the former Soviet Union model, was the location for China's early state-run electronic production, until it was abandoned in the 1980s when the new market economy could no longer sustain such an enterprise. Now, the irony is that the same market-driven economy has found a new but rather fitting colonization for this place.

Avant-garde Chinese artists these days play versatile roles: they produce art works, write their own art critiques, put on shows and sell their own works. Here in Da Shanzi, they have remodelled the factory into galleries and studios, and operate the cafés and restaurants. The large-span factory and warehouse structures, and high sky-windows have been carefully retained, and newly white-washed walls have been adorned with red political slogans from the period of the Chinese Cultural Revolution (1966-1976). Although the whole area has become a colony of freelance and free-spirited artists, the ambience is somewhat sleek and trendy, rather than the bohemian atmosphere prevalent in the countryside artist colonies of the 1980s and early 1990s near Beijing. Its 'place identity' for free artists notwithstanding, 798 is perhaps more reminiscent of the Western-style gentrification of inner city suburbs, as it caters to the emerging young urban middle class in China, as well as serving the Western cultural appetite for the Chinese 'underground'.

Architecturally, the power and simplicity of the structure, and the strong piercing light from the sky-windows, can sometimes overwhelm the art works that are mostly hung on the lower white-washed walls. But the life of such a vibrant community is, too, telling from an architectural point of view, as the 'shell' of the architecture remains unchanged, and the use and the meaning of the same form can be interchangeable. The artists and visitors of Da Shanzi have given new life to this once-dead location, not by radically altering its physical form and fabric, but by a collective will to inhabit it in a different manner. Is this not the secret of meaningful architecture? Demolition of the buildings is planned, despite petitions from the artists and the preparation of a master plan by Bernard Tschumi. It appears that the owners of the site have seen the property's value soar since its makeover, and wish to redevelop to capitalize on the district's success. They will have to wait, as the government recently directed that the 798 Art District be protected at least until the staging of the 2008 Olympic Games.

Right: The art galleries are contained within a stripped down and spruced up factory, originally designed by East German architects in the 1950s.

The factories of the Da Shanzi district found new life in the early 21st century, with the arrival of sculptors, painters and fashion designers, who were looking for cheap space. The district has become a colony of 'cool', with a global reputation. Political slogans from the Cultural Revolution, daubed on the vaulted ceilings, are a permanent feature of the art galleries.

Beijing Books Building

Beijing 2008 (estimated completion date)

Architect Rem Koolhaas and OMA

It is somewhat puzzling that books remain as big business these days - given that the digital world is so overwhelming - and that there is a need to have bookshops concentrated in one mega shopping mall. Rem Koolhaas secured the Beijing Books project after winning the commission for the new China Central Television headquarters. The first phase of the Books project is the construction of the new building, and phase two is to remodel the existing building, which will be incorporated into the new one. The complex is located on the central Xidan Cultural Plaza, and along with the Bank of China building (designed by I. M. Pei) to its west, will define the open plaza.

Koolhaas, a journalist turned architect, rightly deserves the title of an expert on shopping, with a much-publicized Harvard research project on the topic. He sees two critical issues for this project: the problem of what he terms 'introverted shopping'; and the need to communicate the energy of a shopping mall to the outside world. As with the CCTV tower, Koolhaas seems to have been born for this project, for his interest is to communicate (in a journalistic way) the content of the building to Beijing's major street – Changan Avenue - and to Xidan Cultural Plaza. Mega shopping malls these days are sealed and air-conditioned, and the window is no longer relevant, so Koolhaas has chosen to seal the building with large and intricate glass blocks, which serve as internal bookshelves and provide UV protection, as well as decorative external coloring. It appears that some glass panels can be opened, but there is no doubt that the gigantic internal space will rely on air-conditioning. The architect has made an internal 'cross', with two interior streets that open to both Changan Avenue and Xidan Cultural Plaza. The two huge openings are (naturally) entries, but the architect also sees them as 'symbolic windows' to communicate the internal energy to the street and plaza. The 'symbolic window' is indeed the accurate assessment of reality, as the building appears fortified and monolithic, despite these two gigantic, though recessed, 'windows'.

It must be noted that when the architects designed the Great Hall of People at Tiananmen Square, they enlarged the windows and doors in order to give the gigantic building a 'normal' proportion. The architects made a mistake (as with San Pietro in Rome), and as a result of the enlarged windows and doors, the Great Hall of People actually appears smaller than it is, as do the human beings in front of the building. The Koolhaas 'windows' in the Beijing Books Building are also unconventional, but let us hope that they will serve, symbolically, as the 'windows of the soul'.

Opposite: Large and intricate glass blocks seal the building, which faces Xidan Cultural Plaza and Changan Avenue.

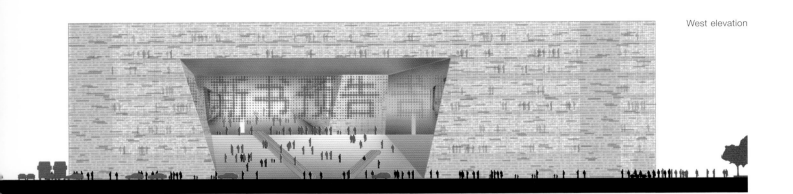

West elevation

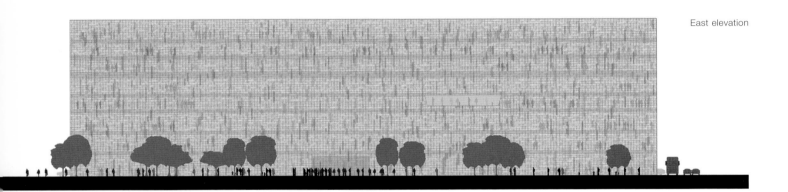

East elevation

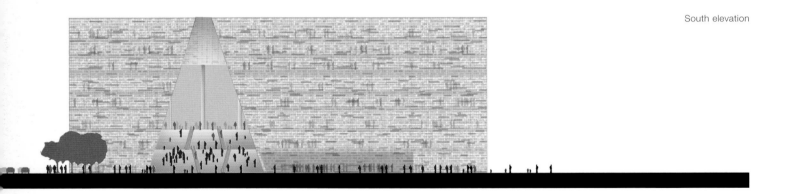

South elevation

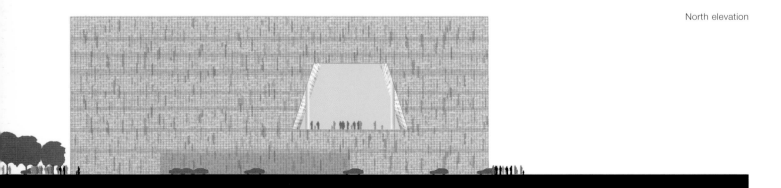

North elevation

Right: The 'best red' study model of the project.

Below: The triangular 'window', seen from Changan Avenue, leads to the internal 'cross' made from two interior streets.

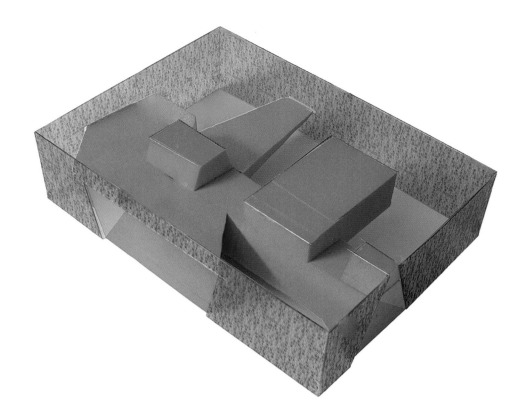

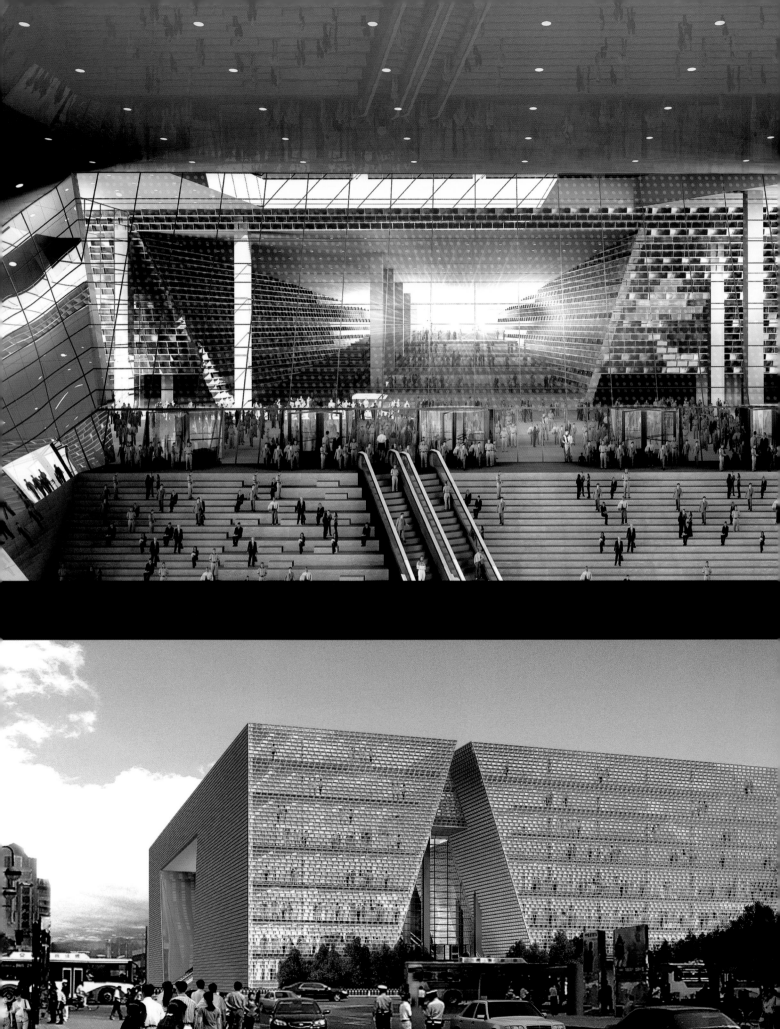

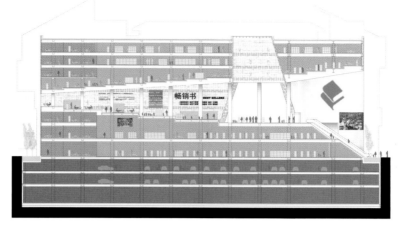

Section

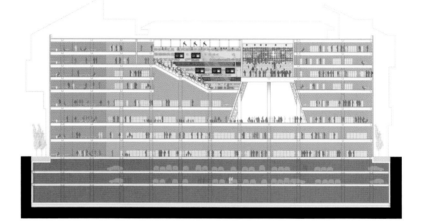

Section

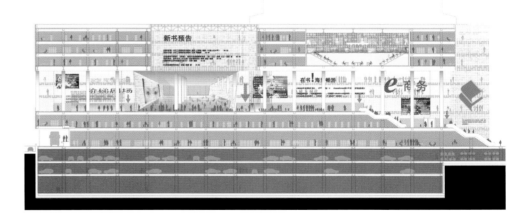

Section

Left: The architect sees
the two huge openings as
'symbolic windows', which
communicate internal energy
to the street and the plaza.

'Watercube' National Swimming Center

Beijing 2007 (estimated completion date)

Architect PTW Architects; China State Construction Engineering Corporation; Arup Group

The name 'Watercube' says it all for the aquatic center currently under construction for the 2008 Olympic Games, as the water-related sports are housed within an orthogonal crystal cell structure. Sydney-based PTW architects, with China State Construction Engineering Corporation and Arup engineers, won the international competition with this instantly legible idea: the three major swimming and water sports complexes are 'carved' out of a three dimensional structural steel frame, derived from the molecular structure of crystal cells. The entire building is a 'space frame' (to use Buckminster Fuller's notion), creating a vivid symbolic representation of crystal and water, as the conventional components of structure – the walls, roof and ceiling – are no longer relevant. Although the three dimensional structure of the 'Watercube' serves as the fabric which covers the major pools, many smaller amenities, such as cafés, are actually accommodated within the 'space frame'.

For architects of an earlier generation, such as Anne Tyng and Louis Kahn, the fascination was not with structural integrity, but with the possibility of such inhabitation within a 'space frame'. Louis Kahn, curiously, was never attracted to the 20th century obsession with transparency, preferring to diffuse natural light into an interior to create a silver shadowless serenity. By contrast, 'Watercube' celebrates the splendor of transparency, which, ironically, is most seductive at night when the opaque box glows… a true crystal fantasy. One cannot help but be concerned with the glare and heat gain in such a 'goldfish bowl' during Beijing's hot summer days, and the architects maintain that these concerns will be eased by the high-tech surface cladding material. The building will be clad with translucent 'ETFE pillows' - an inflated hard plastic - which have superb thermal capacity, as well as providing UV protection. This EFTE skin utilizes a variable shading system, whereby internal foils can be opened and closed to control the light and heat levels.

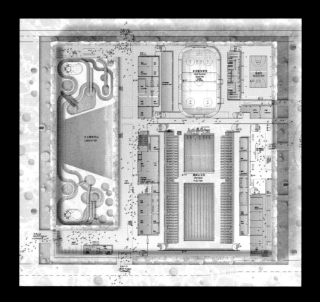

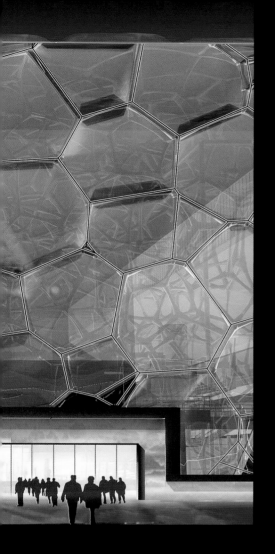

Left: The splendor of transparency is most seductive at night, when the opaque box glows.

Below: The Watercube acts as a greenhouse, with a double skin of 'bubbles' absorbing solar radiation and negating heat loss.

Bottom: Many smaller amenities, such as cafés are accommodated within the 'space frame'.

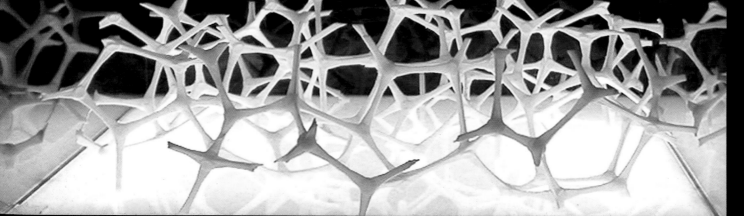

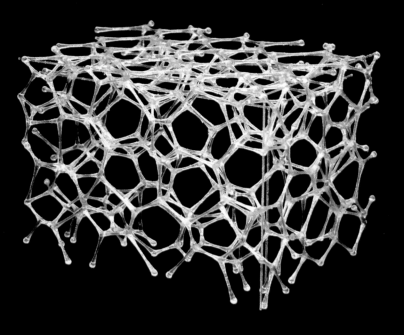

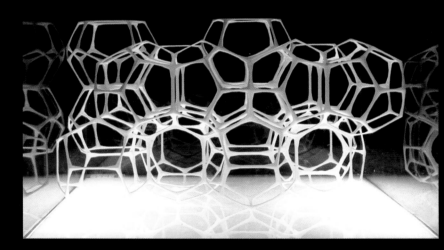

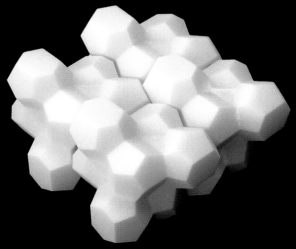

Top left: The entire building is a 'space frame', creating a vivid symbolic representation of crystal and water, as the conventional elements of structure – the walls, roof and ceiling – are no longer relevant.

Left and above: The architecture of the Watercube treats space, structure and façade as one continuous element. The interior spaces appear as a massive cluster of soap bubbles.

Pingod (Apple) Sales/Art Gallery

Beijing 2003

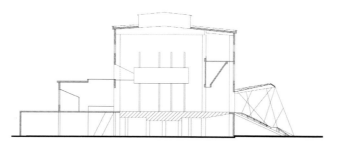

Section

Architect Atelier FCJZ

Pingod is a large residential development of 50,000 square meters, located on the south eastern edge of the Beijing CBD. As with any residential development in China these days, a fancy temporary sales office is an absolute necessity. The architects, Atelier FCJZ, were asked to remodel an existing multi-storey heating plant as a sales office and showroom, as well as a contemporary art gallery. Although this sort of hybrid – property sales and art gallery – is not unprecedented in China, one might think that in this case the idea of combining an art gallery with a sales office originated from the architects. Yung Ho Chang, the principal architect at Atelier FCJZ, enjoys celebrity status in China, and his persuasive capacities and advisory roles behind many projects in China are well known.

The project was planned to be temporary, hence low budget. The design strategy is simple: a multi-storey concrete frame and brick infill building have been cleaned up, with the large internal atrium retained as an art gallery, now defined by dense and colorful light tubes suspended from the roof trusses. But the principal design idea, according to the architects, is the insertion of wedge-shaped boxes into the existing structure. The entry is a large wedge-shaped box that 'sucks' you in, and small wedge-shaped boxes are placed on the upper levels. They were made of translucent glass with a different colour for each, and when lit at night, these 'cinematic windows' revealed the dramas of the building (although recent alterations have obscured this intention). The wedge-shaped forms do remind people of the existing structure in the plant building, but the architects, understandably, call them 'perspectival boxes'. One particular night shot of the building, presumably photographed for publication shortly after its completion, shows female models posing in each brightly coloured box, and their back-lit silhouettes are clearly announced to the outside world. Despite the idea that the art gallery might make the property sales more discreet, or less greedy - a cultural legacy that is deeply rooted in China – the wedge-shaped entry, and more explicitly the wedge-shaped upper level offices which function as shop windows, sent out an unmistakable message that this building is all about sales. The effect of architecture, strangely, often does not match the architect's original intention.

Left: A large internal atrium on the second floor of the original heating plant has been retained as a sales office and art gallery.

Above: Dense and colorful light tubes are suspended from the roof trusses.

Left: The entry is a large wedge-shaped box that 'sucks' you in to the sales office on the second floor.

First floor plan

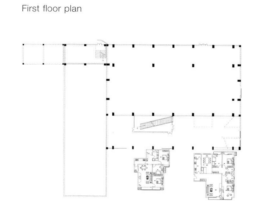

Second floor plan

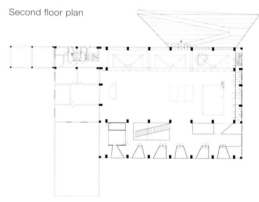

North elevation

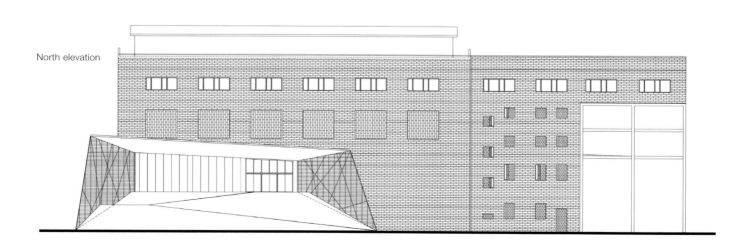

Foreign Language Teaching and Research Press

Beijing 1999

Architect Cui Kai, Beijing Municipal Architectural Design Institute

As far as the 'new architecture' in China is concerned, the Foreign Language Teaching and Research Press complex is 'old'. The office building was built in the late 1990s, and the re-modelling of the printing factory adjacent to the new office was completed in 1999, but when the new office building was erected, the public (as well as many Chinese architects) was quite impressed by its 'exotic' Western look. The building is clad with reddish and roughly textured terracotta face bricks, and the wedge-shaped south east corner entry is extended vertically as a tower to tuck in the staircase, which is echoed with a large triangular façade opening to the internal atrium. Cui Kai is one of the few Chinese 'star' architects who were not trained in the West, but he had opportunities to visit Western countries before he was commissioned for this project. Despite being overwhelmed by the variety of styles in Europe and America, Cui Kai remarked that he was particularly impressed by those buildings that respected the old city fabric. It must be noted that this building does not have much existing city fabric to be 'contextualized', and it is actually more of a Chinese tribute to the red-brick ivy-league campus buildings designed by Robert Venturi in the 1980s. It must also be pointed out that I. M. Pei's 'triangle' in the East Wing of the National Gallery in Washington (1974-1978) was, at the time, regarded as an 'avant-garde' approach by students and young architects in China.

Cui Kai was indeed careful and discreet about the relationship between the new (the office building, which was completed first) and the old (converted from the printing factory on the western side of the new office). Flying bridges connect the two, but they avoid the ancient pine trees on the site. Along with the transparent steel bridge, a large and glazed room on the first level is purposefully designed to enjoy the trees from within the building, and internal bridges penetrate existing walls to connect the different floor heights of the buildings. A seamless integrity is created by the uniform use of red terracotta face bricks and white aluminum window frames, but they do overtake the 'old' - there is not much left but the memory of the printing factory.

Although currently working for a 'mega' state-run design institute - the Beijing Municipal Architectural Design Institute - which has been responsible for much of the city's large-scale institutional fabric, Cui Kai has established his own 'studio' within the institute, and the buildings produced by this studio do carry his personal signature. Despite his independence, Cui Kai no longer produces 'contextualized' works in red brick, nor does he dance between new and old. Sleek and minimalist boxes are just too irresistible, and his contribution to the Commune by the Great Wall (included elsewhere in this book) is one example. It seems the Communist state machine cannot kill artistic integrity these days, but fashion might!

Left: View from the south east to the office building.

83

Above: View from the east, showing the wedge-shaped corner entry tower and a sky-bridge running above the internal atrium.

Right: The geometry of the internal atrium plan reflects the triangular opening in the eastern façade. The building can be seen as a Chinese tribute to Robert Venturi's 1980s campus buildings and to I.M. Pei's East Wing of the National Gallery in Washington (1974-1978).

Gediao Sales Office

Beijing 2003

Architect Wang Hui

Architect Wang Hui was a key player at the Atelier FCJZ under Yung Ho Chang before he became independent, and it appears that Wang Hui has carried on Yung Ho Chang's mission to create a 'contemporary Chinese architecture'. The Gediao Sales Office has provided the architect with an opportunity to materialize his fantasy of a Chinese garden in the sky, which, according to the architect, would also create a 'bamboo top walk'... as seen in Ann Lee's thriller movie *Crouching Tiger, Hidden Dragon*. Flying bridges and platforms in the sales office hover above the garden at the rear of the ground level.

Sales offices for new residential developments are curious building types in China these days. Along with Yung Ho Chang, Wang Hui designed the Pingod (Apple) Sales Office (2003), which also serves as a contemporary art gallery. The Gediao Sales Office, adjoining the site of the proposed apartments in the southern suburbs of Beijing, is a rectangular building comprised of two parts – a smaller entry volume and a larger sales office space – linked by a mezzanine level 'bridge in the air'. The larger double height rear space is animated by a zigzagging overhead walkway, platforms in the air, enclosed office rooms and a garden on the ground floor, and floor to ceiling glazing on the southern façade. The most distinctive feature of the building is the contrast between this fully glazed façade and the rusted Cor Ten steel cladding (both internal and external) of the entire building. The unpretentious raw materials and the no-nonsense welded and bolted joints convey the impression that this sales office is, literally, like a nursery (the ground floor is a garden, and pot plants are scattered everywhere), which seems to suggest: don't worry about the building itself, the goodies are housed within. This building should, by default, function well as a location for selling real estate.

Right: A suspended walkway zigzags through the double height sales office.

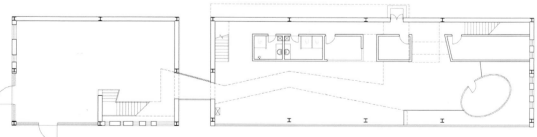

First floor plan

Left: A mezzanine level 'bridge in the air' connects the entry volume with the larger sales office.

Right: The sales office is fully glazed on the southern side.

Below: Rusted Cor Ten steel forms the external and internal cladding of the entire building.

Looped Hybrid Housing

Beijing 2003-

Architect Steven Holl

Although the Looped Hybrid is being pitched as a new urban landscape, as well as a fantasy film city, Steven Holl's loops have a social agenda: the object orientated high-rise housing blocks in Beijing should be interconnected, both on the ground and in the sky. As a residential development accommodating 2500 residents on the third ring road to Beijing's east, Holl has linked the amenities of the eight high-rise residential towers on the ground, and he has also connected them as a loop in the sky... a street in the air with further amenities. Disguised behind the various diamond-shaped and geometric plans, and the angled strips on the façades, the idea of creating communal and public spaces in the sky is not new. In 1946, Le Corbusier conceived the Unité d'Habitation in Marseilles, a multi-level residential block with an internal street, and a gym, playground and other facilities on the roof garden. Another visible expression of the 'sky street' was the unbuilt Golden Lane housing project of 1952 by the British architects Alison and Peter Smithson. Although the concept of the 'sky city' has materialised in some post-war public-housing schemes, such as Park Hill in Sheffield (1957), many remained an architectural fantasy, and the intended 'sky streets' have been largely unused as social spaces. The Unité d'Habitation for a long time was a heavily criticised building due to its abandoned public spaces, but its life has recently returned as 'yuppies' moved in, gentrified the building with loving care, and the 'sky street' is now full of life.

It appears that Holl's clients are indeed visionary, and are willing to invest in this piece of social engineering via architecture. The sky loop is generous enough in floor area to include a café, gym and social club, and the ground level's social infrastructure includes cinema, theatre, hotel and retail outlets. Holl has provided more within the design, as there are more than 200 different types of apartment to counter the homogeneity of apartment living, and all the living rooms and bedrooms in every apartment have been ensured natural light... one hopes that the sociable Chinese will transform the sky loops into lively social arenas.

Right and below: Eight high-rise
residential towers are linked as a
loop in the sky… a street in the air.
The development will accommodate
2500 residents, with amenities at
ground level and in the air.

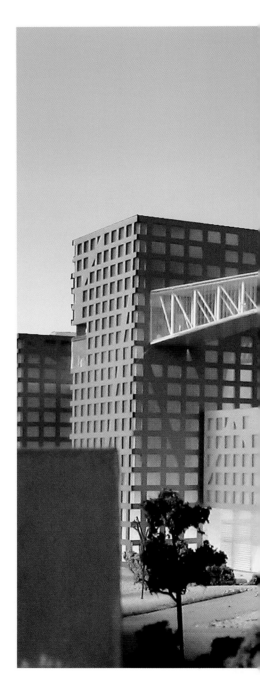

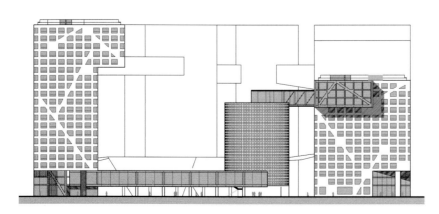

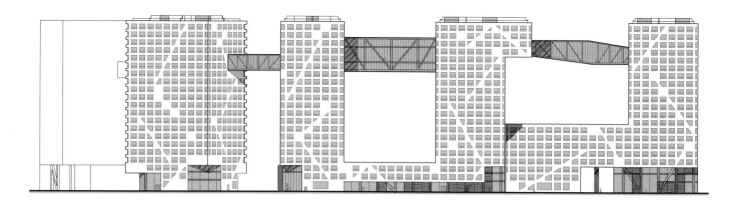

Commune by the Great Wall

Shui Guan 2001-2002

In a recent interview, developer Pan Shiyu revealed that he and his Cambridge University educated wife Zhang Xin have made sufficient money for the rest of their lives… now the agenda of their developments is to leave a mark in history. 'Commune by the Great Wall' does just that! The 'Commune' consists of 11 villas and one clubhouse in a mountain valley near the Great Wall at Badaling, approximately 50 minutes drive from Beijing. The 12 buildings were designed by young or middle-aged Asian architects, and every decision made in the development of the project was tactical, with an international impact in mind. The 'commune' is a *passé* communist ideal for collective living, based upon which the Chinese communist government took away private land ownership and organized farmers into collective living and agricultural production. The Commune by the Great Wall, according to Pan Shiyu and Zhang Xin, is a collection of architectural art, which will ironically serve as an exemplary commune for Chinese individual dream homes, after half a century's collective living. The red star logo certainly adds more cultural currency to the project. Nothing of course has more symbolic capital than the Great Wall, and a site chosen nearby guarantees radiating global impact. Compounding the auspiciousness, rumour has it that 'celebrity' Chinese architect Yung Ho Chang was behind the scenes in selecting the twelve architects from Asia, including himself. Having spent more that 15 years in the USA as an awarding winning 'paper architect' and academic, Yung Ho Chang understands the universal language of the cultural game in architecture, and for some time operated as almost the West's 'single point of contact' when learning about new architecture in China.

The twelve selected architects were Gary Chang (Hong Kong), Seung H-Sang (South Korea), Shigeru Ban (Japan), Cui Kai (China), Rocco Yim (Hong Kong), Chien Hsueh-Yi (Taiwan), Kengo Kuma (Japan), Antonia Ochoa (Venezuela born, lives in China), Kanika R'kul (Thailand), Kay Ngee Tan (Singapore), Nobuaki Furuya (Japan) and Yung Ho Chang (China). The architects were selected, it is said, based on their 'contemporariness' as well as their unique use of traditional material. In the end, not all twelve buildings have used so-called 'traditional materials', but they do look different from each other. Through avant-garde spirit and imagination from these young Asian architects, says Zhang Xin, the Commune by the Great Wall has represented the rise of Asia and China… and the investment and efforts have certainly paid off. Following in Yung Ho Chang's footsteps, the Commune by the Great Wall was selected for the La Biennale di Venezia in 2002, Zhang Xin won the award for the 'Promotion of Architectural Art' from the Biennale, and the architectural models of the project found a place in the permanent collection of the Pompidou Centre. The reason for the project's significance, architecturally speaking

and as succinctly summarized by the La Biennale di Venezia 2002 curator Deyan Sudjic is that '…[the] project, with its combination of aesthetic ambition and the reinforcement of Asian identity through architectural innovation, does that in so many ways.' The 'Asian identity' is displayed more as a regional character in the works than anything else: Kengo Kuma's bamboo and Japanese Zen ambience, Kay Ngee Tan's Singaporean high-tech, Antonio Ochoa's South American colour palette (not even Asian!) and Yung Ho Chang's Chinese rammed earth wall, just to name a few. But the paradox of such a choreographed event may be an acknowledgment that many 'internationally acclaimed' artists and architects – say Damian Hirst or Louis Kahn - are never measured by their regional identity and ethnicity, but against a universal human condition. I wonder whether or not Chinese architects will demand this sort of value recognition in future.

Cantilever House

Commune by the Great Wall, Shui Guan 2001

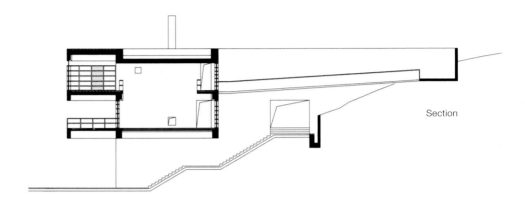

Section

Architect Antonio Ochoa-Piccardo

It is curious to note that the Cantilever House, designed by the Venezuela-born Antonio Ochoa-Piccardo, is often referred as the 'Red House' in Chinese publications. It is perhaps quite reasonable to see the rich and earthy red colour palette as South American, but the Cantilever House does much more than that.

Antonio Ochoa-Piccardo is not an architect who is interested in 'architectural gymnastics'. The architect instead uses a human analogy for his building: if you wish to know about a person, you really need to go beyond their appearance, and see "the light that rises from her flesh" (in the architect's own words). "So be my guest" is the house's invitation, and experience it with your body and mind. The building begins with a stair that cuts into the 'heart' of the house, but to one's surprise, the entire court is a small mountain slope covered with grass. It seems that the red concrete wall and attached ramp are the only man-made demarcations in the landscape continuum of mountain and sky. This landscaped court is more for visual pleasure than actual occupation, as one in fact sneaks into the interior before reaching this point. But the potent juxtaposition between the soft mountain shape, floating clouds, and the hard edge of the architectural walls and ramps, foreshadows what the architect hopes to achieve: a masculine exterior and an erotic feminine interior. An outer layer of space (either enclosed as rooms or open as balconies) is cantilevered from two thick concrete walls to reach out for the mountain and valley views. Although sustaining the warmth and earthy color palette of the exterior, the interior is more refined and delicate with a polished natural wood finish. By contrast, the exterior of painted rough concrete, raw timber panels and stone-made stairs will weather quickly to show its age.

A singular character of this villa is that it possesses 'centers' in its composition - the landscaped court and the double volume living space for example - but they deny any permanent human occupation. Even the large two-level living room is more a circulation node than anything else. The real occupation occurs at the edge, which is cantilevered beyond the two parallel structural walls. The views to the outside are all 'framed', and the open balconies are 'landscape frames', whereas the views from rooms are 'portrait frames' via grid windows. If the building is cantilevered for views, and if it has a human character with 'singing souls', as the architect has promised, let us hope that the 'frame' of this living building, like a human person with a discerning worldview, will enable others to perceive the world as both 'strange and paradoxical'... as once envisaged by Maurice Merleau-Ponty.

Right: The cantilevered structure lifts the house above the hillside. In the words of the architect... "The mountain inside the house. The house in the mountain."

Second floor plan

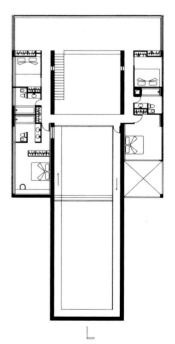

Bamboo Wall House

Commune by the Great Wall, Shui Guan 2001

Architect Kengo Kuma

From the outset, Japanese architect Kengo Kuma established some practical agendas when he designed the Bamboo Wall House. He had no faith in the workmanship of Chinese builders, hence he thought he could only design a 'rough' house. He saw the beauty of roughness in the surrounding landscape, and decided that his building should match that degree of roughness. Kengo Kuma also wanted to learn from the Great Wall, and to situate his building in 'untreated' topography.

But the result is, to my eyes, anything but 'rough'... it is an elongated Miesian box wrapped with bamboo louvers. Perhaps due to its uneven site, the public zone and the bedroom quarter are set in a split section, but the entire building is capped with a large flat roof, which is a little too unsympathetic with the topography of the Great Wall. The public zone is largely glazed, and the central living room - the tearoom - even has a glass roof. This room is symmetrical and slightly elevated, like a stage in a shallow pond, reached by a matt-finished stone pathway. Layers of bamboo louvers wrap and protect this vulnerable and delicate glass box. A bamboo louvered ceiling and bamboo floor make this tearoom a floating island, which is centralized by an enlarged Miesian glass top table (though not quite the Barcelona coffee table). What this centrality definitely lacks is the warmth of a hearth in a house. The Japanese Zen ambience of silence and solidarity (along with my wishful reading of it as an island) in the tearoom make one speculate that the architect has in fact designed a 'Japanese Pavilion' in a Chinese architectural expo (the bedrooms have been designed as *tatami*!).

Mies van der Rohe's Farnsworth House (1951) may be too pure to be useful (as suggested by Colin Rowe), but Kengo Kuma has no such problem: he built an enclosed bedroom quarter, and the bamboo louvers then simply serve as cladding on the solid walls, to ensure a stylistic consistency. The architect has designed a bamboo house in Japan, but the Chinese bamboo scaffold (for building construction) convinced him to try a different degree of delicacy, or roughness. It is encouraging to see that the Chinese scaffold bamboos can be used both as light filters and as wallpapers, but as for the light filter... this building makes me wonder why architects these days are more obsessed with 'shuttered' light via a Venetian louver, than with a light beam via an oculus, or the shadowless serenity of Louis Kahn's diffused light.

Opposite: The bamboo-wrapped central living room – the tearoom – is set in a shallow pond.

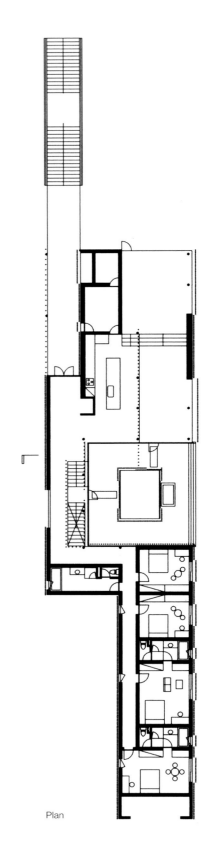

Plan

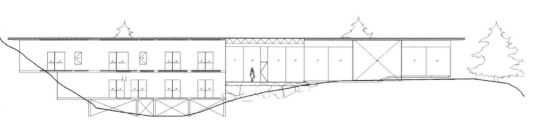

South elevation

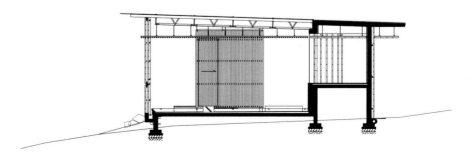

Section

Left: View from the eastern living room to the dining area and the central living room.

Right: The glass ceiling and walls of the central living room are wrapped with bamboo louvers. The floor is also made of bamboo.

Below: The view to the house from the east, showing the large flat roof. Entry to the house is from the north.

Suitcase House

Commune by The Great Wall, Shui Guan 2001

Architect Gary Chang

In terms of inhabitation, the linear house by Hong Kong architect Gary Chang is the most 'unconventional' in the Commune. Although it is not known as the 'Shared House' (a name appropriated by Thai architect Kanika R'kul for her house), the Suitcase House is truly about sharing, for it does not have enclosed bedrooms or fully enclosed bathrooms. Even more unconventional is the lack of clear differentiation between furniture, spatial divisions and floor levels, and the building is fully clad with timber parquetry from inside out, which further enhances the intended blurring.

The best analogy for this villa (it is misleading to name these buildings houses, as they are indeed country villas) is a 'boat' rather than a 'suitcase', as the stratified vertical layers suggest a lower 'cabin' and an upper 'deck'. The lower 'cabin' is a concrete base with 'servant space' – a boiler room, a pantry, bathrooms and a butler's room – as well as a sauna and a library. The upper 'deck' combines sleeping, living, cooking, working and entertaining, and the entire floor can be configured as one huge room by folding back doors suspended from the ceiling. In this scenario, the primitive connotation of the *datongpu* (the Chinese term for a large shared sleeping bed) is materialized... perhaps the true meaning of a country villa in an emerging capitalist society is for family members and friends to be encouraged to 'crash' on a big floor. The original, carefully choreographed, photos of the 'Suitcase House' show semi-enclosed scenarios: sunken floor alcoves partially shelter individuals who are either tapping on a laptop or meditating, and I cannot help but see this as a fascinating coexistence of a primordial brotherhood and 21st century hip. Yes... most windows and the roof terrace have a view of the Great Wall, but who cares about that? This building is an internalized architectural experience.

Left: The cantilevered villa is fully clad with timber parquetry, both externally and internally.

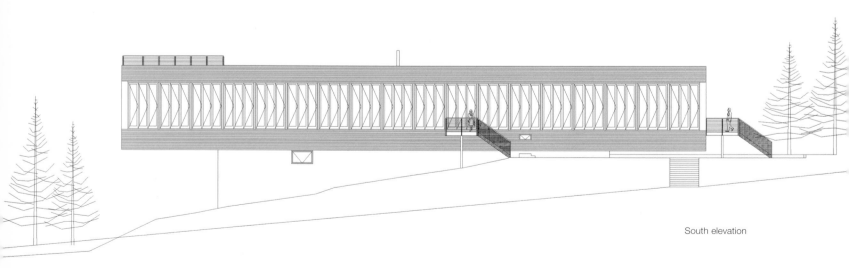

South elevation

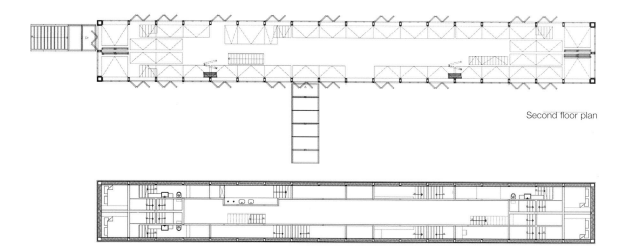

Second floor plan

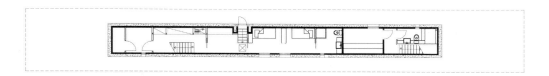

Second floor 'sunken' plan

First floor plan

Left: The entire floor of the upper 'deck' can be configured as one huge room by folding back doors suspended from the ceiling.

Right: The Suitcase House can be literally unpacked... 'sunken' bathrooms, bedrooms and private alcoves are revealed by lifting the floorboards.

Shared House

Commune by the Great Wall, Shui Guan 2001

Architect Kanika R'kul

At the Commune by the Great Wall, Thai architect Kanika R'kul has projected a post-capitalist Chinese society where only a weekend away in a grand country villa can serve as an effective remedy for the alienation caused by money orientated success. If the architect is correct, the holiday villa should be designed to encourage family members and friends to share and to interact, as they will have had so little time for each other during the week. Unlike a Chinese courtyard house where the court is a shared communal space, or the 16th-century Italian villa where the rooms are an interconnected matrix without corridors, Kanika R'kul has designed a 'communal' bathroom quarter, and it appears that between the enclosed 'bathrooms', there are open washbasins. It is indeed curious to see that the architect has chosen to experiment with 'sharing' in this area, for a 'naturalist' mentality could be the least desired Western product for the Chinese in their race for Modernity.

Corridors, a product of the 19th-century English concern for privacy, are inevitable, but here they are wider and more numerous than necessary, with fixed seating and movable furniture scattered throughout corridors that should encourage sharing. The long dining table, which is the norm in the West, suggests the sharing of food, but although Medieval in its appearance, the Western dining habit of commanding a kingdom of one's own culinary set is not about the sharing of food... the Chinese, of course, dining at a round table, actually do share food. Roof terraces and open courts are extensions of the corridors, but they also orientate the sharing of mountain valley views.

This villa is a modern villa, not only with its white-washed Modernist look. Geographer Yi-fu Tuan, in his old age, often recalls the great Chinese house of his childhood, where friends came to share a dinner prepared by the housewife, and after dinner played Majiang on the same dining table until late at night. The housewife said to their friends: "I am feeling a little tired and would like to go upstairs to take a nap, but you all please keep playing..." now I wonder whether that Chinese housewife would be able to turn this sleek white-washed modern villa into a messy and warm house for sharing.

Right: Viewed from the north east, the house is a modern villa with a white-washed Modernist look.

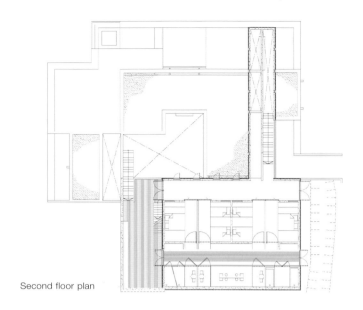

Second floor plan

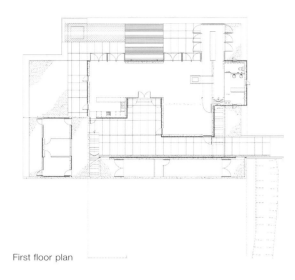

First floor plan

Right: A spacious ground floor corridor with fixed seating.

Far right: A ground floor courtyard leads to a stairway, which accesses the roof terrace.

Left: View from the north, showing the villa's eastern entry, large glazed ground floor living areas and roof terrace.

Right: View of the stairway above the eastern entrance.

Airport House

Commune by the Great Wall, Shui Guan   2001

Architect   Chien Hsueh-Yi

Despite the architect's claim that, as the building is made of local stones, it is in itself a 'wall', this villa, instead of blending into the mountainous site, stands out with its gutsy and un-compromised shape. The 'Airport' House is dominated by a 'thick stone wall', which contains the circulation areas and bathrooms, and the main rooms project from both sides of this 'thick wall'. Understandably, the architect wanted to make this villa appear as a small portion of the nearby Great Wall, but perhaps the building is not long enough, or the structure is not organic enough, to 'follow' the Great Wall's unlevelled topography. Although the architect uses a zoomorphic analogy of the 'spinal column of a living creature', the house appears more like a robot than a living thing. The Great Wall, on the contrary, does resemble a large snake slithering over the ground.

The bedrooms and the kitchen of the villa are neatly arranged in a parallel fashion on the west side of the 'wall' as the quiet zone, whereas the public zone projects out on the east side of the 'wall' as three radiating 'arms'. Of all the villas at the Commune, the Airport House has the most legible readability, as the shape and appearance of the building explain its spatial organization. This is the only building at the Commune that does not have a 'center', and one is tempted to see this villa as one would John Hejduk's wall houses, within which, and unlike a normal house, the hearth, or the center, has disappeared. In a Hejduk wall house, there are only two sides of the wall, and the wall cannot be inhabited. By the same token, in the Airport House you are not meant to linger in the 'wall'… it is for circulation only. It is perhaps, therefore, anomalous that the architect has created a 'transitional corridor' between the 'wall' and the three public rooms on the east side, which is heavily 'designed' with a featured sky-window ceiling and a fully glazed wall for viewing. But it is reasonable to assume that this corridor has not been designed to be the hearth of the building. This villa is named 'Airport', perhaps due to its resemblance in plan to an airport terminal, but it must be true that a building without a hearth (or a heart) could only be an airport, for its purpose is to accommodate transition.

Opposite: Three radiating 'arms', containing the living areas, project from the eastern façade of the 'thick stone wall', which contains the circulation areas.

Left: The stone wall, built from stones collected on the site, forms a 'spinal column' within the house.

Below: The protruding 'arms', resembling those of an airport terminal, seen from the east.

Right: View through the central 'spine' into the dining room.

Plan

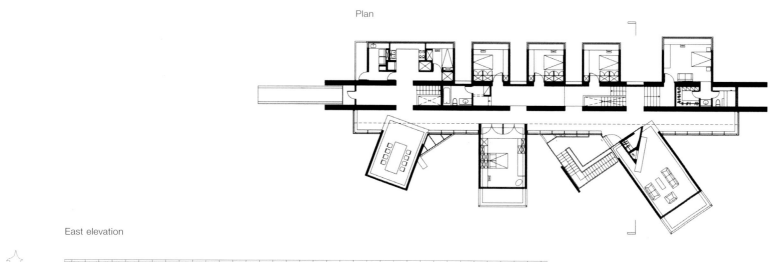

East elevation

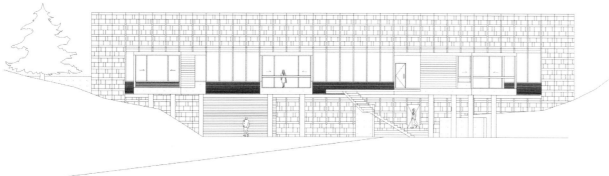

"See" and "Seen" House

Commune by the Great Wall, Shui Guan 2001

Architect Cui Kai

After the completion of his well known Foreign Language Teaching and Research Press Building (Beijing, 1999), Cui Kai appears to have made some major shifts with this "See" and "Seen" villa at the Commune by the Great Wall. No face bricks here - the crisp clean-cut forms and the metal panel cladding suggest some of sort of 'tectonic' tendency ('tectonics' is the current buzzword among the leading young architects in China). A close reading quickly reveals that the 'true-to-structure/material' appearance is nothing more than an architectural disguise of the designer's free will – the exposure of the two-layer skin construction for the master bedroom has not been carried through into the entire bedroom component - as has always been the case in the history of architecture, and we need only to recall the 'faked' structural and material logic of Mies van der Rohe's Barcelona Pavilion (1929). The point, however, must be that the building and its architect should not be judged by the look of the building alone. The "See" and "Seen" villa is a result of the architect's enduring sensibility, which was already evident in his Foreign Language Teaching and Research Press project.

Cui Kai realized that the location of the "See" and "Seen" House can be seen by other villas on higher sites, so he lowered the major part of the building's ground level, with a sloped roof as a 'retaining wall', which is envisaged to be covered by grass. The visible part of the building is an elevated linear bar containing all the bedrooms, with the master bedroom projecting out to 'see' the mountain valley view. The architect argues that, despite its pointed gesture, this elevated bar follows the run of the mountain range, and therefore poses minimal visual impact on the site and the surrounding landscape. Perhaps subconsciously, the architect has imagined a life drama through his real and instrumental language (the spatial disposition and its hierarchy in this villa) whereby a wealthy patron couple, who occupy the master bedroom with the best view, entertain their artist protégés on weekends... long gone is the austere and egalitarian commune life. It may be that the lifestyle implied in this villa, and in this commune, is that which is now being imagined by the emerging and cultured nouveau riche of China.

Right: View from the north, showing the master bedroom at the end of an elevated linear bar.

114

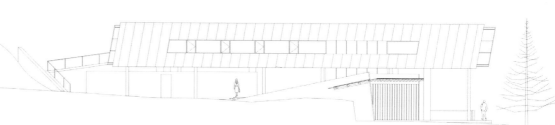

East elevation

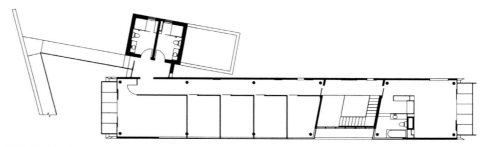

Second floor plan

First floor plan

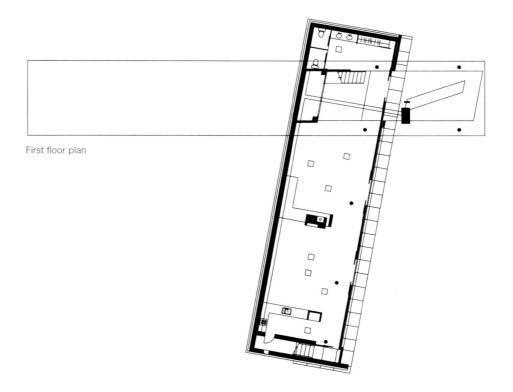

Left: The linear bar, containing the
bedrooms, is raised above the
ground floor of the house, which is
roofed by a grassed 'retaining wall'.

Split House

Commune by the Great Wall, Shui Guan 2001

Architect Yung Ho Chang, Atelier FCJZ

Yung Ho Chang's contribution to the Commune by the Great Wall is the so-called Split House. Well known for his obsession with Chinese courtyard houses, and Beijing quadrangle houses in particular (due to his upbringing in Beijing), Yung Ho Chang has utilized various forms of courts and light wells in his conceptual schemes, as well as in his built projects, since he commenced practice in China in 1996. He describes it as 'micro-urbanism', whereby the courtyard as a building type offers the convenience of natural light and ventilation, as well as a certain degree of centrality, whilst a high urban density is ensured. For Yung Ho Chang, this self-imposed mission of creating a 'contemporary Chinese architecture' has also turned to the 'intimate' ambience of a courtyard house, specifically the small-scale light well courtyards of southern China... culturally coated with potency when the incense is burning.

The Split House is a single free-standing dwelling that is literally split in the middle, and hence, as a gesture, embraces the mountainous landscape. It is still, arguably, a courtyard house except that the court is 'enclosed' by the *Shanshui* – the Chinese notion of landscape, meaning 'mountain and water'. An ideal study or artist's studio should be located and designed to ensure 'the entire landscape is covered by one's eyes' (*shanshui jinshou yandi*) from within. The Split House indeed invites the *Shanshui* to enter: a tiny stream meanders into the entry and runs under the glass floor, and the existing trees on the site have been kept as part of the 'courtyard'. The 'Chinese-ness' of the house (according to Yung Ho Chang) also results from the two thick and heavy rammed-earth walls and lightweight timber structural frames. Of course, this sort of structural and material system has been widely used in various parts of the world, but its labor-intensive technique makes it too expensive for architects in industrialized countries to contemplate. The gentle intrusion into the landscape and the tactile delights of the raw materials notwithstanding, it would be naïve to believe that the two thick rammed-earth walls will make this building ecologically successful in terms of its thermal performance.

Compared with its 'highly designed' neighbors, this building has a certain 'frontier' quality that has been carried through into the interior. This quality is tantalizing, for one must wonder what kind of 'retreat' life is to be accommodated in the Commune. The organizational disposition in this house is a 'normal' modern house, with grouped private rooms mainly on the upper level, and open plan living and dining on the ground floor. But when the living and dining areas are 'split' by the open space, what kind of impact will this 'split' have on domestic life? And how will the open space created by the split 'engage' with the living and dining rooms? Are these conundrums that are yet to be contemplated by the architect?

Right: View to the western entry in the 'split', which divides the house.

Opposite: The living area of the northern wing, looking out to the triangular courtyard.

Right and below: Views of the southern wing show the lightweight timber structural frame and the rammed-earth wall.

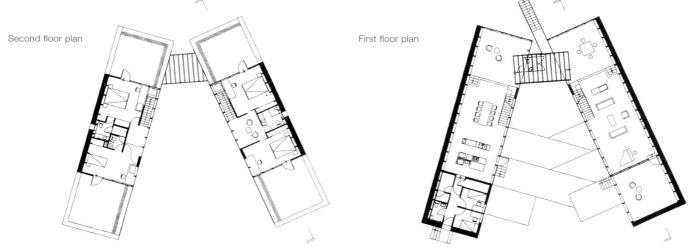

Second floor plan

First floor plan

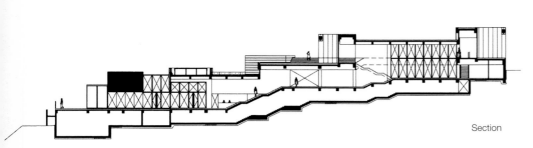

Section

The Clubhouse

Commune by the Great Wall, Shui Guan 2001-2002

Architect Seung H-Sang

South Korean architect Seung H-Sang is ambitious, and clearly wished to set the world to rights when he designed the Clubhouse for the Commune at the Great Wall. Although the building, which is the largest in the Commune, looks like a purpose driven Modern building with its various components, the architect argues that it is designed as the opposite. Seung H-Sang believes that the Western faith in rationality and science is largely responsible for the kind of architecture that is determined by a purpose, which architecture must serve and accommodate: 'form follows function' as the Modernist doctrine says. Leaving this generalization aside – Modern architecture, as we already know, can be as mysterious as that of the pre-Modern period, and the spatial disposition of this clubhouse does appear to have the potential to be flexible.

The architect has introduced a Korean notion of 'emptiness' in a house – *madang* – to the design, and this 'emptiness' does not have to serve any purpose. The Clubhouse consists of several horizontal 'bars' arranged to follow the site's contours in a parallel fashion. The homogeneous linear indoor spaces, and the outdoor spaces in-between, form a matrix of rooms and outdoor courts that can be used for all sorts of purposes. Following this tendency, the architect also (naturally) claims to have maximized the public spaces and minimized the private ones. It is, though, somewhat ironic to see that one feature of the design is a series of private dining areas as found in a Chinese restaurant: these dining areas are divided into separate rooms, with each facing a thematic outdoor garden. The building has a 'formless' feel, for none of its shapes explicitly suggests its use. Predominantly clad with Cor Ten steel panels, the Clubhouse hopefully will weather gracefully to blend itself into its surroundings, as with its neighbour, the Great Wall – a ruin open to all imaginations.

Right: View to the Clubhouse entry from the south.

Shanghai World Financial Center

Shanghai 1994-

Architect Kohn Pedersen Fox Associates

A high-rise tower is first and foremost a figurative motif, and the architects Kohn Pedersen Fox understand this only too well. The World Financial Center, designed by KPF, will be recognized and remembered instantly, due to its distinctive geometric form as well as its height. Located in the Lujiazhui Financial and Trade Zone in Pudong, this 492-meter high, 101-storey building was planned to be the tallest in the world, but that race is now wide open. The tower begins with a square footprint, but the square 'column' is intersected by two sweeping arcs, which see the square tower diminish to a single line at the apex. As the thinness at the top makes the floor plans difficult to use, the architects cut a huge circular opening through the building, and it has also has been argued that this is necessary for relieving wind pressure. An axis was drawn from the Shanghai television tower - the Oriental Pearl – thus the size of the circular opening in the World Financial Center is to be the same diameter as the 'pearl' on the television tower. Among its high-rise neighbors, the pure geometry of the tower's form does make it stand out. The use of the building, naturally, is predetermined by the geometry: surprisingly, the architects found that the lower floors were good for offices, and when the upper floors were narrowed by the two sweeping arcs, they are suitable for hotels suites.

Across the river from the Bund of old Shanghai, the Lujiazhui area has been designated as 'the' Asian financial center, and the World Financial Center project began in 1994 when the seed of the iconic Shanghai Opera House was also embedded. Now more than 10 years have gone past, and the project, after a five-year suspension, is still under construction, while the Shanghai Opera House has been a proud symbol for the city for some years. The 1997 Asian economic crisis aside, one of the reasons for the interruption in construction was a figurative reading by some Chinese architects that could not have been expected, even in the wildest dreams of the building's architects. Japanese money is backing the project, and the design was viewed as an image of two Japanese military swords holding a Japanese flag in the sky of Shanghai - a painful memory in a not-so-remote history. Ingeniously, the architects responded to this public outrage by placing a bridge within the circular opening, and in so doing, claimed it as a Chinese moon gate. Despite such an inauspicious beginning, the World Financial Center promises to redefine the Pudong skyline. The question then arises: does a tower actually function for any other reason than defining a city skyline? The tendency to internalised space in Foster and Partners' Jiushi Tower across the river in Shanghai might, as one example, animate the social life of its inhabitants in a high-rise tower, but the image of Foster's tower is very subdued in comparison to that of KPF.

Left: The square column is intersected by two sweeping arcs, which see the tower diminish to a single line at the apex.

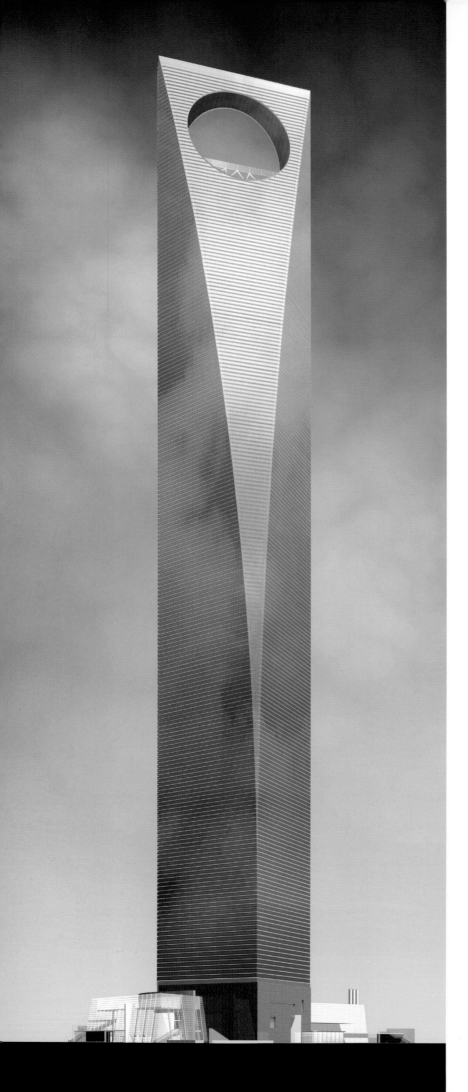

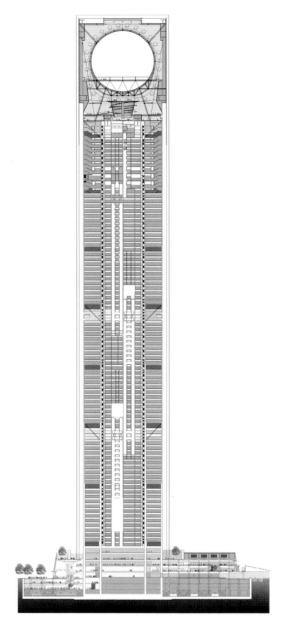

Section

Left and above: As the thin-ness at the top of the tower made the floor plans difficult to use, a huge circular hole was cut through the building, providing a memorable figurative reading.

Right: The pure geometry of the tower's form creates distinctive profiles.

Jinmao Tower

Shanghai 1997-1999

Architect Skidmore, Owings and Merrill; East China Architectural Design and Institute

Any survey of 'new architecture' in China in the past two decades would be incomplete without the Jinmao Tower. Completed in 1999, this 420.5 meter high, splendidly shining tower stands on the Pudong bank of the Huangpu River. Directly opposite the Bund – the city silhouette of old Shanghai – the Jinmao Tower has not yet been surpassed (the controversial 101 storey World Financial Center is only now being erected in the same area) as a symbol, representing what the Chinese may achieve in the race for the Modern – the best and the tallest! Perhaps more significant than its height is the number of floors... an auspicious 88 storeys. Eight is phonetically similar to 'making a fortune' in Cantonese, and in the early 1980s when affluent Hong Kong was the role model, Deng Xiaoping praised the entrepreneurial southern Chinese with the epithet 'being rich is glorious'. Subsequently, the number 8 has been universally admired through telephone numbers, vehicle plates and any numerical component of a building.

The Jinmao Tower rises abruptly from its 'pencil point' footprint, like a Buddhist pagoda. In fact, the architects wanted the building to recall a Chinese pagoda, and the footprint appears as a replica of the Liao dynasty (AD 1056) Buddhist timber tower in Yinxian, Shangxi province. The podium, as a consequence of such a concentric footprint, is separate from the tower, and the precinct around the site is designed as a compound with a landscaped courtyard, reflecting pool and seating. This 'retreat' is isolated from pedestrians by heavily trafficked roads. The building does look remarkably business-like... perhaps it is not meant to be easily accessible to every one in the street.

The entire complex has a floor area of 278,800 square meters, incorporating a hotel, offices, restaurants, retail, conference and exhibition halls. The first 50 storeys are office space, below the 38 storeys of the 555 room Grand Hyatt Hotel. The hotel has an enormous 152 meter high atrium, dubbed a 'time capsule' due to its elaborate interior lighting design. On the auspicious 88th storey is a restaurant with views to old Shanghai over the Huangpu River. Understandably, the building is equipped with the most advanced building system, structural engineering and communication technology, and its glorious façade seems to prove just that! The entire glass curtain wall is decked with an intricate metal 'skin', which reflects daylight with an ever-changing metallic sheen, but this skin does not let the fenestration 'breathe'. There is no resemblance to the tectonic elegance of a Chinese timber pagoda, other than the 'pencil point' footprint, and its illuminated night image is more reminiscent of the Art Deco Chrysler Building. In the race for the highest building, this resemblance provides a sense of déjà vu... of the tall tower race in early 20th century New York.

Right: The Jinmao Tower rises abruptly from its 'pencil point' footprint to an observation deck and restaurant on the 88th floor.

Concept sketch

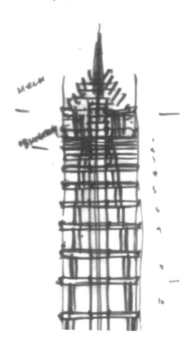

Left: The entire glass curtain wall is decked with an intricate metal 'skin', which reflects daylight with an ever-changing metallic sheen.

Above: The entry to the tower is isolated from pedestrians by heavily trafficked roads.

Shanghai Pudong
International Airport

Shanghai 1999

Until the new Beijing International Airport is completed for the 2008 Beijing Olympic Games, French architect Paul Andreu's Shanghai Pudong International Airport will remain as the most glorious airport in China. The race for the best airport has been a parallel competition with that for the tallest building, but the airport competition seems to have intensified after the September 11 tragedy, for cities now have to think twice before they put up tall iconic buildings. In the Asian region, we have seen the splendid Hong Kong Airport (1998) by Foster and Partners and its immediate rival, Kuala Lumpur International Airport (1998) by Kisho Kurokawa. Despite the obvious fact that Kuala Lumpur will not overtake Singapore to become the economic and cultural center of South East Asia in the foreseeable future, the Malaysians still went for grandeur with a much over-estimated capacity. Of course, neither Beijing nor Shanghai have such a problem: the current Beijing International Airport was only completed in 1999, and its capacity is already stretched. This airport race, however, could be much inflated in China's regional cities.

Selected from six invited international competition schemes, Paul Andreu's winning entry, is not surprisingly, seen as a 'seagull' ready to soar into the sky. This indeed is what the city of Shanghai wants to see... Shanghai is ready to spread its wings! Perhaps not as sculpturally fluid as those 'big bird' concrete airports designed by Eero Saarinen in the 1950s and 1960s (the TWA Terminal (1962) at Kennedy Airport in New York for example), this lightweight and transparent 'big-shed' is exuberantly glittering at night. Located at the mouth of the Yangtze river, the Pudong International Airport is planned to have marine links with a new harbor, which is to be artificially constructed to the east of the airport site. The airport is about 30 kilometers from the city center, and is linked to the city with a magnetically levitated high-speed train.

Unlike Foster's longitudinal arrangement in the new Beijing International Airport, Andreu has followed a parallel design, emphasizing the logic that the distance between check-in and departure should be minimized. The large-span internal space is covered by full ceiling lights composed of struts with small skylights at the top of each light tube. This sea of 'stick' lights is reflected on the polished granite floor, and the entire indoor space appears to be sandwiched by pointed 'acupuncture needles'. Needless to say, the ceiling lights are an acclaimed design feature, but I am a little surprised that this 'prickly' ambience has been accepted by the Chinese clients as a theme of harmony. The ingenious structural solution - holding the massive roof with cables and adding the weight to the roof by pouring cement into steel pipes - should be seen as the key artifice of this building.

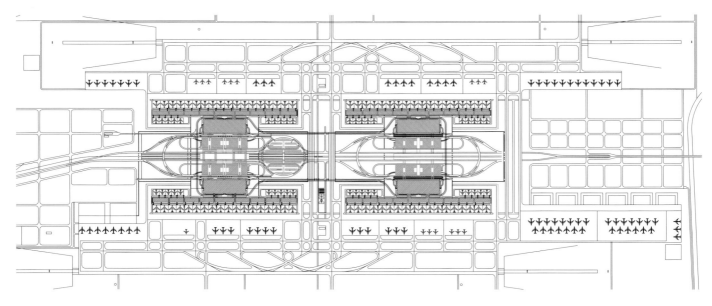

Plan

Above: The Shanghai Pudong International Airport is seen as a 'seagull' ready to soar into the sky.

Left: The large-span departure hall is covered by full ceiling lights composed of struts with small skylights at the top of each light tube.

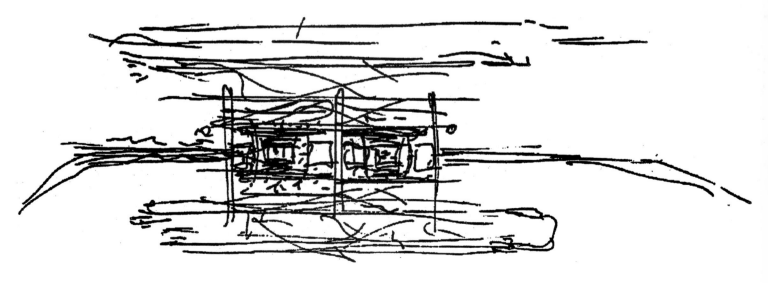

Concept drawing

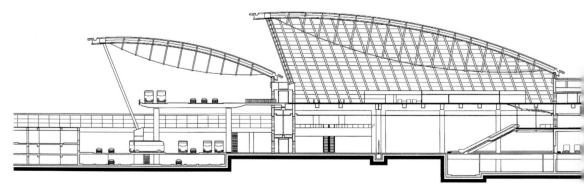

Section

Left: View of the drop-off zone for departures. The ceiling lights are an acclaimed design feature, but the ingenious structural solution of holding the roof with cables and adding weight by pouring cement into steel pipes, should be seen as the key artifice of this building.

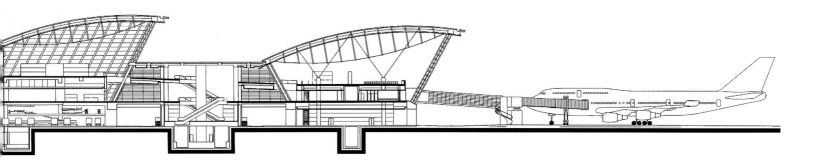

Shanghai Opera House

Shanghai 1994-1998

Architect Arte Jean-Marie Charpentier et Associes

The Shanghai Opera House opened well before the National Grand Theater in Beijing, and has been the precedent for the 'opera house race' in Chinese cities. Indeed the symbolic capital that the Opera House has given to the city of Sydney is desired by every major city aspiring to be a global player. Another precedent established by the Shanghai Opera House is the implementation of the widely recognized Chinese cosmic model of round heaven and square earth. Above the major theaters, which are housed within square boxes, the two upper level floors are contained in a large curved plate, which appears as a 'big roof', often associated with a pre-modern Chinese building. Crude though it may be, this figurative motif is easily understood as an image for the city. By contrast, the symbolism of the National Grand Theater in Beijing, which is perhaps a subconscious imitation of such a cosmic model, remains obscure.

The big 'roof', like a Chinese timber temple, serves at least one practical purpose: it casts much needed shade for the fully glazed square buildings below. There are three state-of-the-art theaters – the grand theater of 1800 seats, a medium-sized theater of 600 seats and a small theater of 300 seats – plus rehearsal rooms and facilities, a concourse and various amenities, which even include a shopping mall. The grand theater is claimed to have the world's best-equipped stage setting for ballet, orchestra and opera, with all-purpose acoustics and lighting. The iconic character of the Shanghai Opera House has proven to be popular, so perhaps it is what it is... a role model for the civic decorum of contemporary Shanghai.

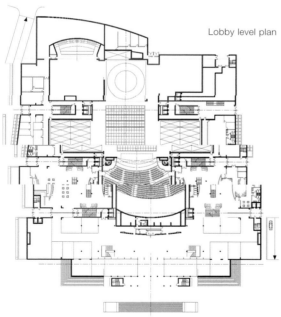

Lobby level plan

Left: The large curved plate of the roof provides shade and protection for the fully glazed square buildings below.

Above: The grand theater is claimed to have the world's best-equipped stage setting for ballet, orchestra and opera.

Right: View of the south-facing lobby areas.

信息中心
global resources
INFORMATION CENTRE

China Europe International Business School

Shanghai 1995-1999

Architect Pei Cobb Freed and Partners

Even after I. M. Pei's retirement, Pei Cobb Freed and Partners have carried on the Pei legacy. The China Europe International Business School in Shanghai is not extraordinary, but it is a piece of architectural work with 'quiet eloquence' and considerable skill, which is rarely seen these days when the 'architectural gymnastics' are so tempting.

The campus occupies a level 4-hectare site, with 34,203 square meters of floor area. As this is a size that is sufficient to form a self contained urban fabric, it must have been a conscious decision to 'fortify' the campus with building blocks and lines of trees 'against' its light-industrial neighbours. The advantage of this micro-urbanity is two-fold: vehicles are kept out of the campus, with access to various parts of the campus from the periphery; and the contained open spaces are sensibly organized into quadrangle courts with surrounding colonnades, as every university campus surely aspires to have a decent quadrangle, better still with a clock tower. The appropriate scale and ambience of an academy is not the only design intention: instead of sandstone and ivy, the buildings are rendered with white-washed walls and inlaid with charcoal brick stripes. This is a language that Pei developed with his Fragrant Hill Hotel (Beijing, 1983) in order to evoke a resonance with the private gardens in his hometown of Suzhou. As with the Fragrant Hill Hotel, the Suzhou garden elements of weeping willows over reflecting pools and of diamond shaped windows for view framing are seen in the quadrangle courts. A more 'learned' reference is the central library building, which is surrounded by reflecting pools. This is not easily decipherable as a motif from Pei's hometown, but it is a prototype of the classic Chinese library in literature: in a water pavilion, books are protected from fire. This notwithstanding, an 'island' library is indeed the ideal place for reading and contemplation.

Left: View from the campus entry to the central library building.

Site plan

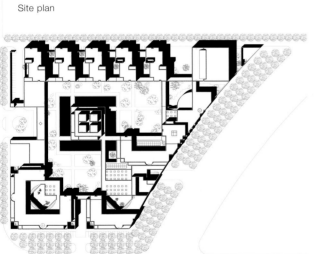

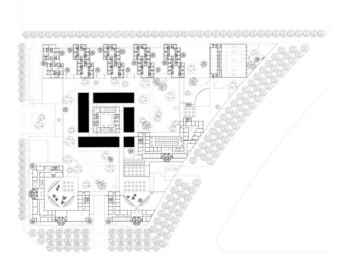

West elevation

Above: The campus presents a self-contained urban fabric, with 'fortified' building blocks viewed over reflecting pools.

Opposite and left: The quadrangle courts and colonnades provide the scale and ambience of an academy. The white-washed walls with inlaid charcoal brick stripes are a continuation of the language developed by I.M. Pei at the Fragrant Hill Hotel (Beijing, 1983).

145

Jiushi Headquarters

Shanghai 1995-2001

Architect Foster and Partners

The 40-storey Jiushi Corporation Headquarters building sits on the south Bund of old Shanghai. Among its colonial neighbors, it is un-apologetically modern, and compared with the 'beauty contest' of the new high-rise developments across the river in Pudong, this building appears calm and austere. It is, however, by no means ordinary.

Jiushi Corporation is one of Shanghai's largest investment companies, but it was no small feat for the company to conceive of and to build this headquarters. The result of an international competition-winning scheme, it was the first Norman Foster building in mainland China, and the result is a highly intelligent and computerized modern office complex of a world standard. A Foster building can never be cheap of course, but of greater importance is that the spatial and structural configuration of this building has the lucid clarity that one can find only in Foster buildings. The symmetrical fan-shaped tower footprint addresses the corner site with a courtesy much needed in the current Chinese urban context. This same shape also ensures that the tower can be easily held up with periphery columns, thus maximizing the useable floor areas, with a concrete lift core on the south side. The tower and the adjacent 6-storey building have a layer of colonnade that echoes the urban context of the Bund.

The real bonus resulting from the clarity of the building's configuration is an internalization rarely seen in high-rise towers these days. 'Sky gardens' on the north side of the tower between levels 15 and 17, and between levels 26 and 28, are used as social spaces for the office workers, and a much celebrated 'winter garden' on the top is a 6-storey atrium with stepped back terraces of office space on one side. The animated façade notwithstanding, the glamorous and leisurely ambience of these internal 'sky gardens' does, one hopes, increase the productivity of the office workers.

Published *parti* sketches of the building are to be found on British Airways Club World notepads, which makes one wonder whether or not this is the reality of 'highflying' architectural practice these days: buildings are actually designed on airplanes or in travel lounges. Despite the fact that many architects are no longer working on drawing boards, these sketches are a reminder that architecture is still a laborious and time-honored craft.

Right: The northern façade displays a calm austerity in the context of contemporary Shanghai.

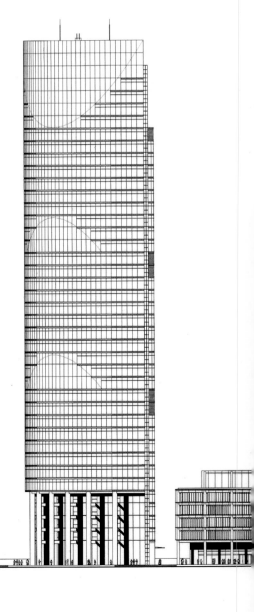

146

Right: View of the western façade.

Section

First floor plan

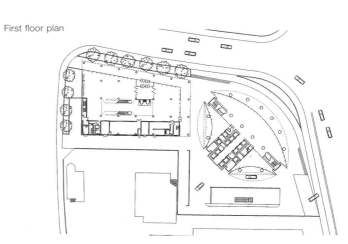

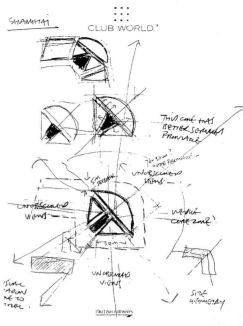

Top left: Viewed from the new Pudong business district, the Jiushi tower sits at the southern end of the historic Bund on the western bank of the Huangpu Jiang.

Above: Two terraced 'sky gardens' open up the office spaces on the northern edge of the building. A six-storey wintergarden forms an atrium at the top of the tower.

Left: The fan-shaped tower is supported by peripheral columns, which maximize the usable floor space.

Building C, College of Architecture and Urban Planning, Tongji University

Shanghai 2004

Architect Zhang Bin and Zhou Wei, Tongji University Research and Design Institute of Architecture

Building C is an extension to the old Building B of the College of Architecture and Urban Planning at Shanghai's Tongji University. Tongji University has long been associated with German universities, so it is perhaps no surprise to see a little Bauhaus resonance in this calm rectangular building, which has a bookend glass staircase tower and is vertically marked with large abbreviations of the college's name (in English). 'Recession' seems to be the character of the building's southern façade on its campus side, as the windows are recessed behind balconies, and the building is grounded and recessed on the first three levels to face a sunken outdoor court. This subdued 'recession' is rare these days in China, but it signals an architectural pursuit of social space from some young practitioners, as well as a level of sophistication in their achievement.

The 'recession' into the earth has resulted in a sunny outdoor court leading to the entry, which encourages social mingling. This architectural framing of sociality is then internalized with a generous double-volume public room above the entry. Unlike most buildings, however, the social space does not stop here – it penetrates deep into the building through a 'grand' sky-lit staircase that reaches every level. The architects and the clients for this building were even more visionary than that, as multi-level atriums were inserted into the building on the northern side, making the north façade more transparent and animated than that of the south, and a roof garden completes the sequence of social spaces.

The building for a school of architecture inevitably serves as a 'role model' for future generations of architects, and one hopes that the civic character of this building will make an imprint in the minds of students, even if it remains a tacit message. For their peers, the architects have sent out a clear message through a small palette of materials (concrete, glass and stainless steel panels)… the simplicity of architecture has a noble goal, which is to frame social life.

Right: View of the glass staircase tower, and the southern and eastern façades.

Left and above: Multi level atriums were inserted on the northern façade, creating a more transparent and animated elevation than that of the south.

Third floor plan

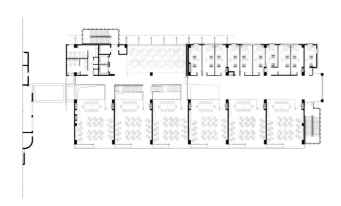

First floor plan

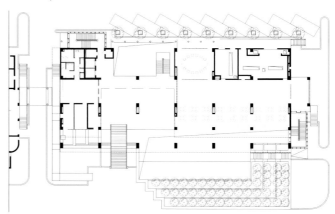

Above: A grand sky-lit atrium and staircase reach every level in the building.

Right: The 'bookend' glass staircase tower is vertically marked with large abbreviations of the college's name (in English).

Zhang Bin and Zhou Wei, Tongji University Research and Design Institute of Architecture

Elevation

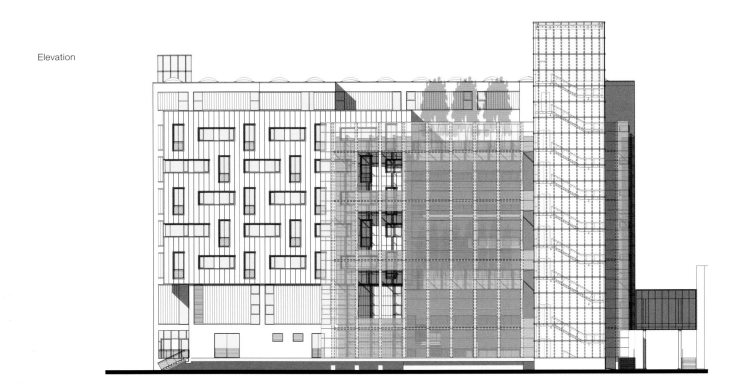

Elevation

Zhang Bin and Zhou Wei, Tongji University Research and Design Institute of Architecture

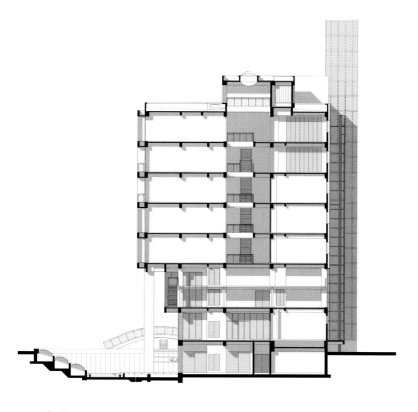

Section

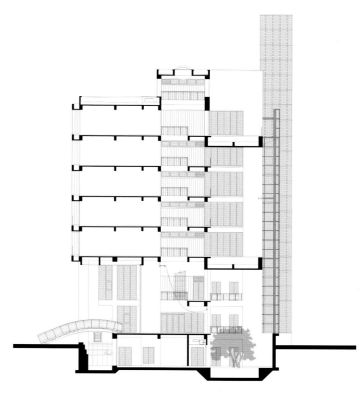

Section

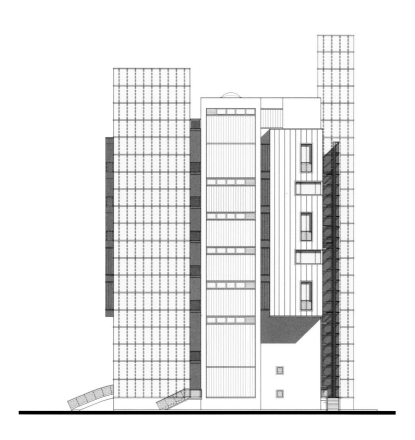

East Elevation

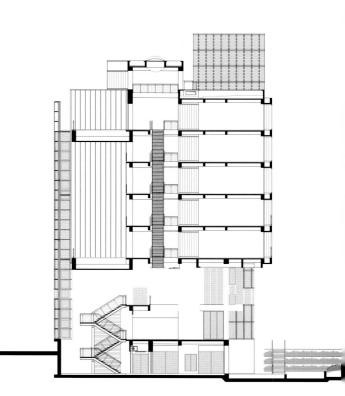

Section

Tongji University Library Remodelling

Shanghai 2003

Architect Wu Jie and Tongji University Architectural Design Institute

The remodelling of Tongji University Library provides a good example of recording time and memory in architecture. The preservation and careful remodelling of old buildings make little economic sense in China, as anywhere else, for it often costs more than knocking down the old and building the new. Increasingly architecture is becoming 'consumable' due to the use of non-lasting materials and fashion cycles... especially evident is the fast 'turnover' of business in retail buildings, where the interior fit-outs are constantly restyled to reflect trends. This fact notwithstanding, buildings still cost substantially more than any other consumable product, both in labour and in energy, so they are still expected to last much longer. Institutional buildings, in particular, carry the history of the institute, as well as the memory of its people. Tongji University Library, located on the campus main axis, is just such an iconic institutional building, serving as the background for the Chairman Mao statue facing the main gate.

The architects have carefully retained the first phase of the library, built in the 1960s with quality brickwork, which set the tone for the symmetrical and axial centrality for the library on campus. The twin towers in the library quadrangle were built in the 1980s, resembling two gigantic trees with an impressive (more than 8 meters) cantilever from the two structural cores. It is claimed that the great cantilever was to showcase the superior engineering capacity of Tongji University - well known throughout China. All the windows in these two towers have now been replaced with clear glass, a crisp touch that matches the newly remodelled western component and glass oval lobby in the quadrangle. The western end building, which was built in the 1990s as the most recent addition to the library, has received major 'surgical' work, with a steel frame and louver-look 'skin' wrapping the building mass and exterior stairs. The language is coherent with the glass and steel oval lobby within the quadrangle and beneath the twin towers, which is centred with a circular translucent glass reception desk. All of which, needless to say, forms a sharp contrast to the old masonry. Judging from the current speed of development, the Tongji University Library may need another extension some time soon. It is tempting to speculate that this new addition may be altered next time, as the sleek steel and glass will not age as gracefully as the masonry of the earlier buildings. The dust and soot produced by the Shanghai's revitalized economy could render this part of the building most unattractive, and furthermore, unlike the crafty brickwork of the 1960s and the mighty structural gesture of the 1980s, this trendy addition carries little Tongji history and memory.

Right: A louvered steel frame has been wrapped around the western section of the library.

First floor plan

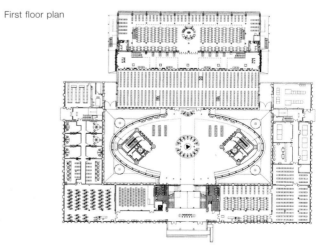

Above and right: The louvered façades of the remodelled western section of the library.

Left: A sleek glass and steel lobby has been installed beneath the towers built in the 1980s.

Above right: The atrium space between the western section and the earlier components of the library.

Xintiandi

Shanghai 2001

Architect Wood and Zapata; Nikken Sekkei; Tongji University Architectural Design and Research Institute; Skidmore Owings and Merrill

The Xintiandi redevelopment, comprising restaurants, cafés, galleries and boutiques, has created a new popularity for outdoor eating in Shanghai – a trend that soon spread to other Chinese cities. Xintiandi (meaning 'new heaven and earth') is explicit in its determination in setting trends, despite initial doubts from the Shanghai Government, investors and potential renters. The area was an old *Linong*, a uniquely Shanghai urban housing prototype that can be seen as a high density 'middle ground' between the English townhouse, or terrace house, and the southern Chinese courtyard house. They range from one to three bays, and as with the terrace house they share common walls. The 'courtyard', literally known as 'sky well', is pushed to the front, serving as the entry and the light well. *Linong* formed the residential city fabric in Shanghai from the early 20th century, and many still remain, but they have not been upgraded for more than half a century.

The Shanghai *Linong* are architecturally eclectic, they follow a typical pattern that begins with a neo-Classical Western-style entry and front façade, which are complemented with a simplified Chinese Deco interior. One wonders whether or not this says something about Westernization in China, but if nothing else, this *Linong* pattern surely is the material evidence of what the city of Shanghai has comprised since the mid 19th century. Shanghai (meaning 'the upper sea') is dubbed as 'the sea that absorbs one hundred rivers', and the city has taken pride in this aspect of its cultural character since its colonial days... Shanghai takes on anything! The market-driven economy has made it impossible to preserve the *Linong* by upgrading them as houses, so commercial development *a la* Xintiandi is the way to go. Even then, the developer (the Hong Kong based Shui On Group) had to gamble that the Chinese would be attracted to outdoor dining, and that the costly exercise of literally preserving the 'skin' of the old would be eventually paid off by its cultural capital.

The architects have been successful in carefully 'paving out' what appear to be the natural civic pedestrian alleyways and plazas. The paved and landscaped outdoor areas have been made inhabitable with the help of the shops, restaurants and cafés that open up to them. Only a handful of buildings with historical significance have been 'preserved' in a strict sense, most of the buildings have been 'gutted' to be fitted out with fashionable interiors, or occasionally extended with glass volumes. The current Xintiandi occupies only two city blocks, and is already backed by new and large scale commercial buildings and a park with an artificial lake. A much larger second stage development is on its way, and Xintiandi, understandably, is the core and the draw-card for future developments in the area. While much of the historical city fabric is being knocked down elsewhere in Shanghai, as well as in other Chinese cities, due to the raw economic formula, the Xindiandi development has saved a *Linong* district by following the same formula... as long as we are content to preserve the 'shell' alone, and allow the 'content' to be changed. Shanghai, once again, has proved that it can take on anything, and do so with confidence and style.

Left: The restoration of traditional Shanghai *Linong* was a case of literally preserving the 'skin' of the old.

Left and right: The architects have successfully paved 'out' what appear to be natural civic pedestrian alleyways and plazas. The developer had to gamble that the Chinese would be attracted to outdoor dining, and that the cost of the exercise would be paid off by its cultural capital.

Site plan

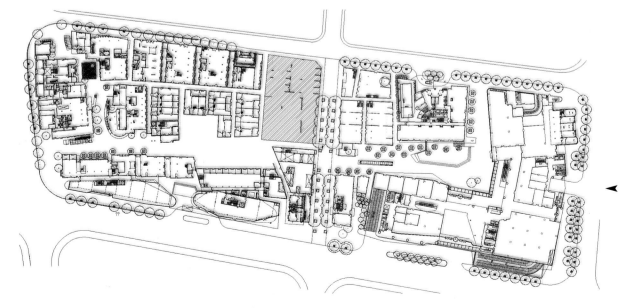

Left: Xintiandi is the drawcard for future developments in the area. While much of Shanghai's historical fabric is being knocked down as part of a raw economic formula, the Xintiandi development has saved a *Linong* district by using the same formula… the content is changed, but here the 'shell' remains.

West Lake Southern Line Pavilions

Hangzhou 2002

Architect Zhang Zi and Zhang Ming, Original Design Studio

The West Lake Southern Line Pavilions are a series of two storey lightweight structured pavilions, connected by walkways through the trees. Their lakeside location is viewed as delicate and fragile by the architects, for the West Lake of Hangzhou is regarded as a supreme natural beauty, and has always been coated with Chinese literary legends. Leisure activities, such as a tea room and café, are accommodated within the pavilions, and architects Zhang Zi and Zhang Ming established several rules at the outset for the design: the structures should not be overtly aggressive, instead they should be made deliberately fragile to match the delicate landscape; they should be 'ordinary' rather than unique or avant-garde; and they should not be nostalgic, nor carry any historical burden.

In a few of the small projects included in this book, a group of young architects appear to be consciously creating a counter force to the architectural 'beauty contest' currently being fought among the large architectural firms, local as well as international. It is rather noble of Zhang Zi and Zhang Ming not to reference the style of a Chinese pavilion, given that it is a well-established type of architecture that serves only to allow the body and mind to meander in the landscape. The style of a Chinese pavilion is neither neutral nor formless; it is, to my frivolous imagining, like a flower. But once within, the windows and screens, often shaped like flowers as well, are carved out of white washed walls and provide uncompromising picture frames for the landscape. Despite their refinement and delicacy, these new pavilions in Hangzhou are, ironically, framed by the trees and water, and due to their openness and transparency, they do not provide a semblance of the internal experience of a classic Chinese pavilion. It is unknown whether the architects were influenced by recent Australian 'critical regionalism' of finely crafted timber, steel and lightweight flying roofs. But if not, I am tempted to speculate that the Chinese escape from heavy historical and cultural baggage (which Australian architects do not possess) has resulted in some common ground. I am also tempted to speculate further that 'critical regionalism', as popularised by Kenneth Frampton, may have ironically created homogeneity, which in itself is not necessarily a bad thing.

Left: The structures were designed as fragile components of the delicate lakeside landscape.

Above and right: The project comprises a series of two storey lightweight pavilions connected by walkways through the trees. The structures were designed to be neither avant-garde nor overtly historical.

Site plan

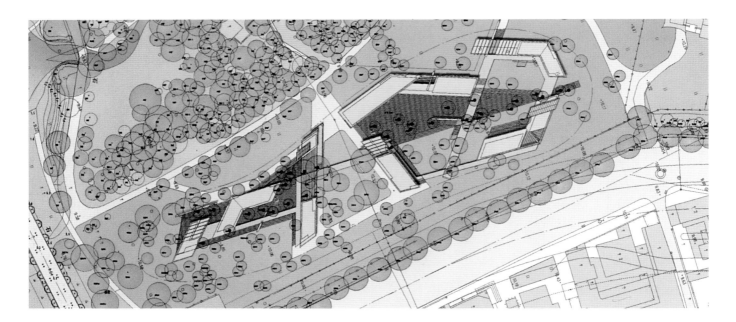

Left and above: The openness and transparency of the finely crafted timber and steel structures bear no resemblance to the style of the traditional Chinese pavilion.

Tiantai Museum

Tiantai, Zhejiang Province 1999-2003

Architect Wang Lu

In the current context of architectural exuberance in China, architect Wang Lu, who is also a professor of architecture at Beijing's Tsinghua University, has been able to maintain an analytical attitude towards architecture. Among the works included in this book, the Tiantai Museum could perhaps be seen as a 'dated' piece of work in the ongoing race for 'newness'. Located near Guoqing Temple on the southern range of Tiantai Mountain, the museum was designed with little concern for style or trends. Regarded as the origin of the first Chinese remodelled Buddhist branch (*tiantai zhong*), Tiantai Mountain is the site of pilgrimage for many Buddhists from as far as Japan, Korea and South East Asia. To build a modern museum in such a place enriches the cultural life of locals as well as visitors, and this is an encouraging trend in some of the provincial cities in China.

Although the neighbouring Buddhist City has its recognizable Buddhist temple appearance and far-reaching radiating visual impact, the architect choses to see its internalization as the primary character of a Buddhist temple – a fortified 'clean oasis' (*jing tu*) away from the world of the profane. The Tiantai Museum does indeed recreate this tranquil oasis by fencing itself off from the busy road to the east with a long stone wall. Behind this stone wall, two types of exhibition space are arranged in parallel fashion either side of open courts, and the elongated museum complex gradually opens to the Chuxi river, which bounds the site on the west. A significant decision by the architect was to emphasize horizontality, which is enhanced by the rough stone wall on the east. Instead of competing with the big roof of the Buddhist City, this stone wall, as well as the flat-roofed museum rooms hidden behind it, quietly addresses the splendour of the Buddhist City, like an essential ingredient designed to 'pull out' the flavour of the place. The discernment of the site, or the *topo*, by the architect makes it difficult to label the museum as an example of Frampton's 'critical regionalism', for the architect has made conscious 'selections' of the character of the *topo*: decisions that are cultural as well as ideological. The use of local stones and bricks, and the skilful response to the physical site, are regional, but they are by no means 'critical'. The building completes the site with its acknowledgement of a universal paradox that, according to the architect, is of type and *topo*.

The type is a museum design, that of the universal, and the *topo* is the architect's reading of the cultural landscape, that of the region. As for the type, Wang Lu separates the exhibition spaces as 'volumetric' rooms for objects, and 'panel' rooms for hanging pictures. The arrangement of these rooms is based on the idea of having the choice to enter one of them, instead of journeying through a linear sequence of all rooms. To correctly design exhibition spaces, lessons can be learned from the history of museum design worldwide.

Left: The museum, viewed from the south east entry, with the Tiantai mountain range in the background.

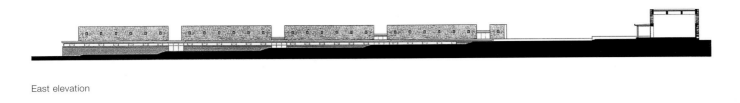

East elevation

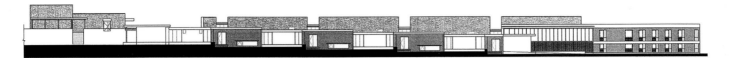

West elevation

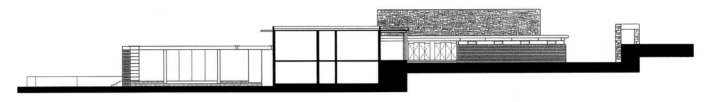

Section

The linear approach, for example, was challenged by Austrian architect Hans Hollein with a configuration of four gallery rooms divided by a cross corridor, so when standing at the centre of the cross, one can choose to enter any one of the rooms. Wang Lu has used open courts, and rooms-within-rooms, to provide the choice of entering the rooms. Of course, one has the choice of not entering any of the rooms, but of lingering in the riverside courts in order to admire the view, and this configuration, naturally, is also a response to the site. Although the stone and brickwork will weather gracefully, the architect has admitted that the steel columns are less refined, due to a lack of understanding from his local collaborators. But whether or not the inhabitants of this museum will understand the playing out of the paradox of the universal and the local, and whether they will embrace this building with collective loving care, remains a much larger challenge.

Right: The design emphasizes horizontality, which is enhanced by the use of long rough stone walls.

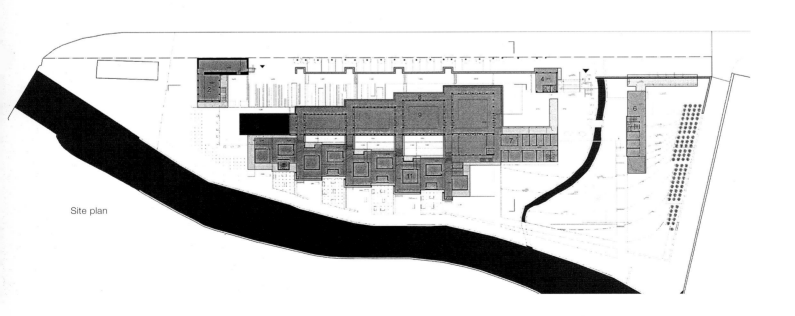

Site plan

Above and right: The usual linear
sequence of progressing through
the rooms of a museum is replaced
by an arrangement of open courts
and rooms within rooms, which
are utilized to provide a choice for
the visitor.

Opposite above: The low-lying
forms of the museum, seen from
the north west, with the Buddhist
City as a backdrop.

Wenzheng
College Library

Wuxian, Suzhou 2001

Architect Wang Shu, Amateur Architectural Studio; The
Architectural Design and Planning Institute of Suzhou
Construction Group

Nothing could have been more of an ideal commission than a
university library for the architect, as he had prepared for this
opportunity for many years. Since his student days, Wang Shu had
been deeply torn between rebelling against a non-questioned
tradition and his sense of an almost missionary cultural obligation.
He belongs to a generation of young Chinese architects who received
an American version of quasi-Beaux Arts training in the 1980s in
China after the entire higher education system was suspended for a
decade during the Cultural Revolution... (the author is an unworthy
peer of this group). Many of these architects admire European
Modern architecture as a canon – although most of them had not seen
any 'real' Modern buildings until recently – and the self-imposed
mission for some of the more ambitious is to achieve some sort of
cultural specificity in a modern building. The Wenzheng College
Library at the old Suzhou University was one of the first institutional
commissions that Wang Shu and his small Amateur Architectural
Studio received, and the project, literally, is a materialization of the
internal conflict that the architect possessed.

The library is located on an artificial lakeside, and the major part of
the building is thus elevated above the water. This is perhaps the most
powerful character of the library, which gives a double, yet legible,
connotation of a pre-modern Chinese library built on the water for fire
protection, and an idyllic reading pavilion overlooking a lake. Despite
its white-washed masonry walls, flat roofs, and large areas of glazed
façade and skylights, the library has a curiously twisted axis that
marks the entry and ends with a 'pavilion' (a white box with a fully
glazed façade facing the lake), which is named 'the reading room for
poetry and philosophy'. It appears that this axis is the extension of a
road leading to the site, and it also makes, in plan, a connection
between the forested hill and the lake, but in reality there is no visual
link along this axis. There are more 'twists and turns' in the plan, and
not all can be justified within the site, but it is said that Wang Shu
wished to recreate the feel and scale of alleyways in China's southern
cities. The use of large areas of glazing has seen full-height curtains
installed, which begs the question of the character of a library. The
'twists and turns' are visibly expressed to the outside, but internally
the building is a simple shed. Surely the building character of a good
library is a matter of internalisation, which has not yet been addressed
in this building.

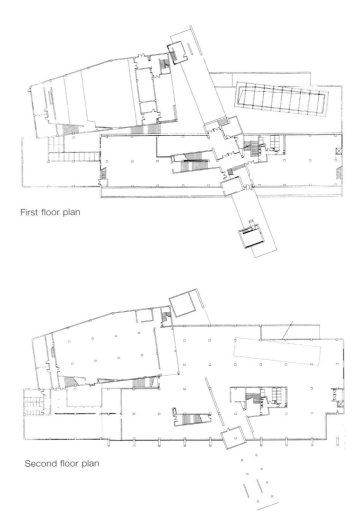

First floor plan

Second floor plan

Right: The lakefront pavilion, referred
to as the 'reading room for poetry
and philosophy' terminates the axis
which cuts through the library

Ningbo Campus Library, Zhejiang University

Ningbo 2002

Architect MADA spam

After returning from studying and working in America, architect Ma Qinyun began his practice, MADA spam, with large-scale projects. His acquaintance with Rem Koolhaas must have well prepared him to cope with a university campus commission, which, from master planning to individual buildings, was all handled by MADA spam, and was built in just over a year. The Ningbo Campus of the Zhejiang University occupies two bands of the entire eight bands that form the higher education zone for the city of Ningbo, also planned by MADA spam. The planning strategy for an instant urbanity, according to Ma Qinyun, is to integrate various uses into parallel 'bands', hence it can begin and finish at any time without concern for 'completion' in order to achieve an urbanity with sufficient density. The two bands for the Ningbo campus are a teaching zone and a residential zone, and between these zones, two large-scale monumental buildings - library and administration - loosely define an open landscaped campus plaza. The sketches from the architects, which seem to come from the hands of Le Corbusier, portray sculptured monumental buildings seen from a distance. The vastness of the space seems quite real, but the views framed by lines of mature trees (from Corbusier as well?) may not be instantly fabricated.

The library, elevated on a large podium, is a nine-storey red cubic building, and as expected, the building has a central void and a solid perimeter. But unlike Louis Kahn's Exeter Library (New Hampshire, USA, 1972), the central void in the Ningbo Campus library is occupied by 'floating' spaces, such as an index room, an internet café and a reading lounge. Despite these floating spaces, illumination from the skylights still passes through and reaches the bottom of the void. The perimeter is solid and filled with book-stacks, and the reading areas are, naturally, 'carved' out from the book stacks and are reflected on the building façades. In Kahn's Exeter Library, the book-stacks form one layer of the perimeter, which is exposed through large circular openings to the void in order to 'seduce' the reader. An outer layer of the perimeter forms the privatised reading areas. For Kahn, the void, symbolically, is about sharing, which complements the private experience of reading and learning. The books, in this scenario, mediate the two experiences. Quite to the contrary, the architect of the Ningbo campus library has followed the notion of a Buddhist scripture pavilion - *cangjing ge* - in a Chinese temple, wherein the library is a sacred room with permanent stacks of Buddhist scriptures. The spiritual power of the scriptures should overwhelm the reader, and hence books are worshipped. It is unclear as to whether or not the architect wanted to make this library a sacred place in a modern university, but its scale, bright colour, podium elevation and the vast foreground lawn contrive to make it the most monumental building on the campus.

In fact the architect does not need to play out his cultural ethnicity in this library design - *cangjing ge* for example - to gain international recognition. In the 2004 exhibition of 'MADA On Site' in Berlin's Aedes East gallery, Rem Koolhaas speculated that Ma Qinyun may become the first Chinese architect to achieve an international 'breakthrough', and he would be warmly embraced and welcomed as 'one of us' - by which Koolhaas surely meant his kindred spirits in the West.

Left: Viewed from the south west, the nine-storey cubic library building is elevated on a large podium.

183

Podium level plan

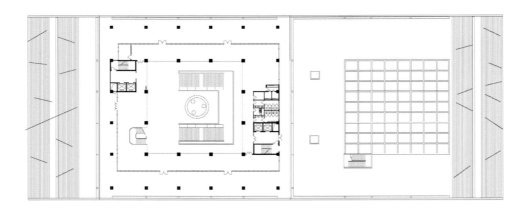

Section

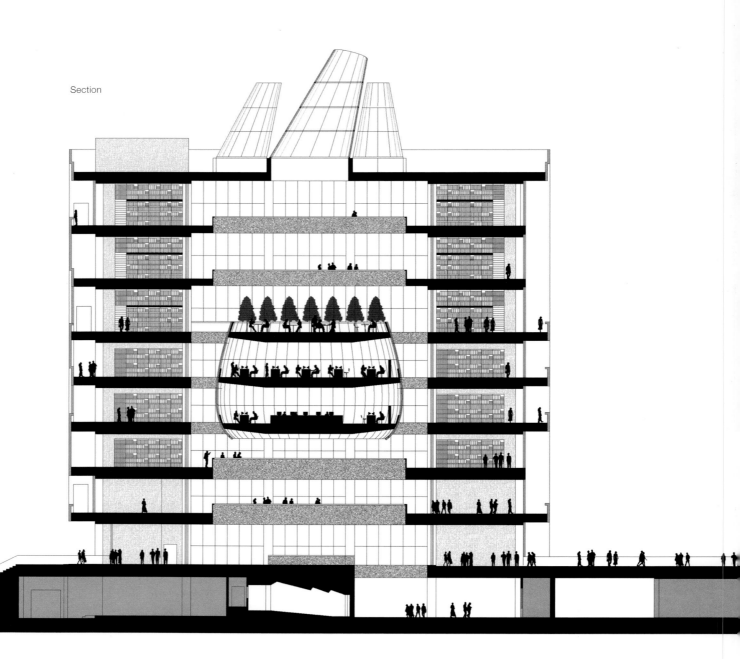

Above: The sculpted monumental
mass of the library, the central
building on the Ningbo campus,
seen from the north east.

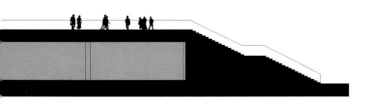

Ningbo Urban Museum

Ningbo   2003

Architect MADA spam

Even in a global city, it is not necessary to have a large museum dedicated to urban history and development, but Ningbo, relying on its international port and a fast growing manufacturing industry, aspires to be a big player in the Shanghai region, if not competing with Shanghai itself. An Urban Museum may have seemed like a better idea than an art gallery, which takes time to build its collection, for Ningbo has a long literary urban history that can be easily fabricated into exhibits to occupy vast floor areas.

The choice of architect appears most suitable: Ma Qinyun of MADA spam, a disciple of Rem Koolhaas, has an interest in instant urbanity in China. Like Koolhaas, Ma Qinyun proved to have the ability to create a mega-scale urban building with an immediate media impact. The museum is a conversion of an old waterfront warehouse building, which (according to the architect) was a post Cultural Revolution building with a 'rationalist' character: a clear structural grid, high ceilings and an almost monumental quality

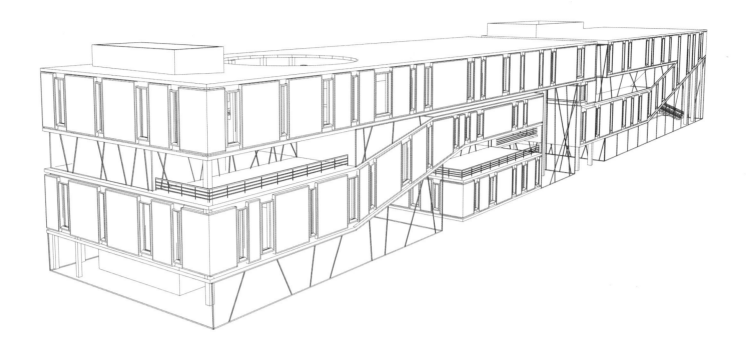

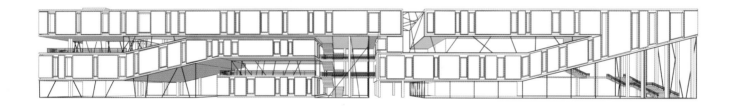

without any cultural or ideological connotation. The architect appears to have appreciated the existing quality of the building, but he has given it a wrap of media connotation: like billboards, the colored glass blocks on the building's surface announce the sloping floors and staircases inside the building. As with a Koolhaas building, the Ningbo Urban Museum has very few enclosed 'rooms'; the entire building is a vertical loop combining the circulation and exhibition space, which the architect calls 'fold'. I suspect that this 'folded' loop may become a little tired if there are no stimulating exhibits to keep people focused.

The night view of the building from the water is suggestive: the colored blocks glow from the internal lights, and make the entire building reflect in the water. The building is like a ship! Perhaps it wanted to be a passenger terminal, or perhaps it wanted to be much larger, like an Archigram structure with flying bridges all over the city...

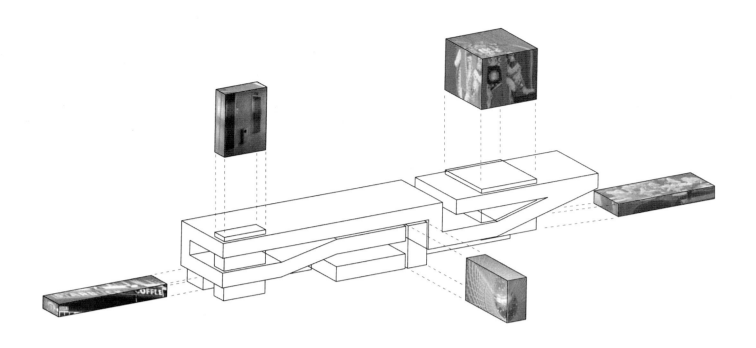

Left and right: The museum is a conversion of an old waterfront warehouse, with a new wrap of colored glass blocks.

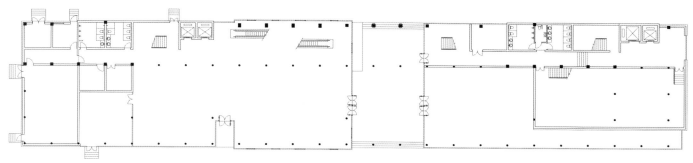

First floor plan

Laowaitan

Ningbo 2003-

194

Also known as Ningbo Y-town, Laowaitan was one of the oldest Bunds and foreign territories in China, established for foreign traders when the port of Ningbo first opened in 1844. Laowaitan, meaning the Old Bund, was in fact 20 years older than the famous Bund of Shanghai. The redevelopment of Laowaitan as a fashionable 'urban village' has occurred, however, after the success of Shanghai's Xintiandi redevelopment. In modern China, Shanghai has, once again, set the trend.

In Ningbo, the architects and urban designers faced a dilemma: on the one hand they wanted to stage a 'vogue living' set, as often represented by the Bund in Shanghai; on the other hand, they wanted to remind local residents that Ningbo pioneered trade with foreign countries through the establishment of one of the earliest trading ports in China. The built result is, quite literally, a clear juxtaposition of the 'old' and the 'new', and the 'old' now comprises newly designed vernacular courtyard buildings suitable as a low-rise and high-density urban prototype. The trend of fabricating 'old' urban markets with vernacular courtyard buildings from the region started much earlier, as shown by the successful redevelopment of the Fuzi Miao (Confucian Temple) district near the famous Qinhuai River in Nanjing. Historically, the Qinhuai River was renowned for its boat brothels and cultivated singing girls, who catered to the literati, government officials and businessmen. This was, of course, abandoned when the communists took the reins of the government in 1949. The whole area was rebuilt in the 1980s with compact vernacular courtyard buildings, which included mainly retail spaces and local food courts, plus some office spaces. This Fuzi Miao redevelopment proved popular, and it was copied all over China, using semblances of regional vernacular building styles. The core of the Ningbo Laowaitan development follows the same pattern – the pristine new brickwork and roof tiles currently look like a stage-set in a film studio – with only a small number of refurbished 'real' old courtyard buildings. But the masonry structure and roof tiles will weather quickly… as with those 19th century brownstone or sandstone neo-Gothic universities in the New World, they will not take very long to become 'old' and 'historical'.

Left and right: The 'transitional' buildings that form the outer core of Laowaitan utilize generous glazing and timber cladding, with a similar scale and silhouette as the inner 'old' buildings.

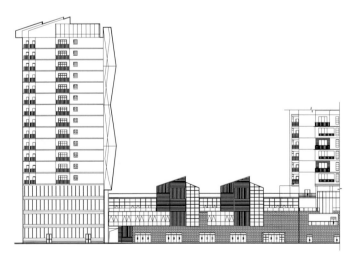

Section

The 'new' at Laowaitan is a legible idea of encouraging citizens to look forward, whilst 'preserving' part of their urban history, and the showpiece will be the waterfront port, which is now being turned into a pedestrian promenade. A major background of the waterfront promenade is MADA spam's 'ultra modern' Ningbo Urban Museum (included elsewhere in the book). Alongside these past and future 'time capsules' lies a layer of 'transitional' buildings, which form the outer boundary of the 'old' core. These buildings, following the same height limit of four to five storeys, have been designed sensitively to the 'old', with a similar scale and sloping roof silhouettes. But these buildings are genuinely new: the generous use of glass and the reddish timber panel cladding announce that they have been designed by architects well versed in the contemporary scene. And what sort of roles do these buildings serve in Ningbo's urban life? The signage on one such reddish building façade says it all... KFC + 'Spring in Paris'. Like a shopping mall, this kind of urban 're-development' creates a fantasy world, it conveys both a nostalgic urban past and a fabrication of ultra vogue and modern. But these projects are infinitely preferable to shopping malls... those mammoth buildings that suck up all the energy from the city in order to provide air conditioning to a completely fortified interior 'wanderland'.

Above: The waterfront promenade between the river and the Laowaitan precinct.

Above right: Comprised of newly designed vernacular courtyard buildings, Laowaitan has been redeveloped as a fashionable urban village.

Right: As with Xintiandi in Shanghai, Laowaitan is envisaged as a stylish entertainment and dining precinct.

Guangzhou International Exhibition Center

Guangzhou 2000-2002

Architect ASX Japan; The Architectural Design and Research Institute of South China University of Technology

Loops that wrap around and inside a building seem to be in vogue - from Rem Koolhaas' CCTV to MADA spam's Ningbo Urban Museum, and to Steven Holl's looped residential towers in Beijing. But why loops? To ask this question may sound unintelligent, as if querying as to why a 4-button suit was preferred over a 3-button one by a fashion critic. And surely each architect has a reason for using the loop. The architects for the Guangzhou International Exhibition Center - a vast building of 500,000 square meters in floor area, and 810 meters in length - wanted to make the building as light as a "wave of breeze" from the Pearl River. So the gigantic silver metal-clad loop that wraps around the building towards the river is the "wind materialized".

Guangzhou has become renowned, since the late 1970s, for its aggressive culture of holding international expositions for manufacturing and products, and this well-earned reputation as a city for commerce had to be matched by a 'mega' state-of-the-art exhibition center. The Japanese architects ASX won the competition, and the project was realized in three years in collaboration with the design institute at the South China University of Technology (such collaboration is the standard procedure for a foreign firm working in China these days). The location is to the east of Guangzhou CBD on the south shore of its famous Pearl River, a site that is well connected by public transport. The architects delivered the state-of-the-art expo facilities, and have arranged them with a clear logic: the entire plan is divided into 9 bands, 90 meters in width. The first stage of the project has realized five of these bands, plus an entry band on the east. As they all belong to the same curve looping towards the river, layers of landscaping from the river to the building have been created. When the 450-meter long fountains are activated in front of the building, it is envisaged that the entire structure will float and dissolve like a breeze from the river. This, of course, can only be possible when the building is viewed from the north bank of the Pearl River. In reality, the elaborate entry platforms and stairs around the building do not convey the image of a feather lightly touching the ground. The entry pavilion along the eastern end of stage one, with its overtly looped supporting structure and curved roof, asserts itself as an aggressive 'dragon' (as intended by the architects), which actually contradicts the elegant metaphor of a breeze from the river.

Right: View from the north east, showing the massive sinuous entry pavilion.

Left: View from the south west, showing the silver metal-clad loop which wraps around the building.

Right and below: The entry pavilion at the eastern edge of the building asserts itself as an aggressive 'dragon', as intended by the architects. The silver loop, which encloses the building itself, is designed to make the structure as light as a 'wave of breeze' from the Pearl River.

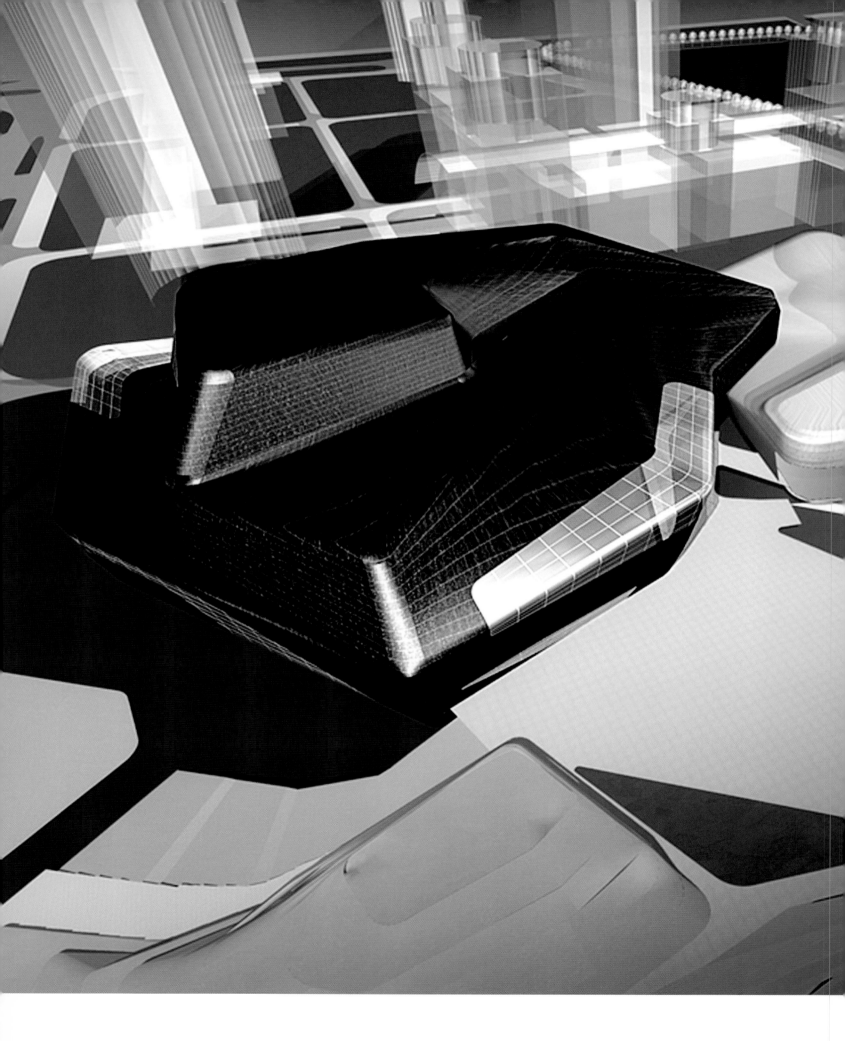

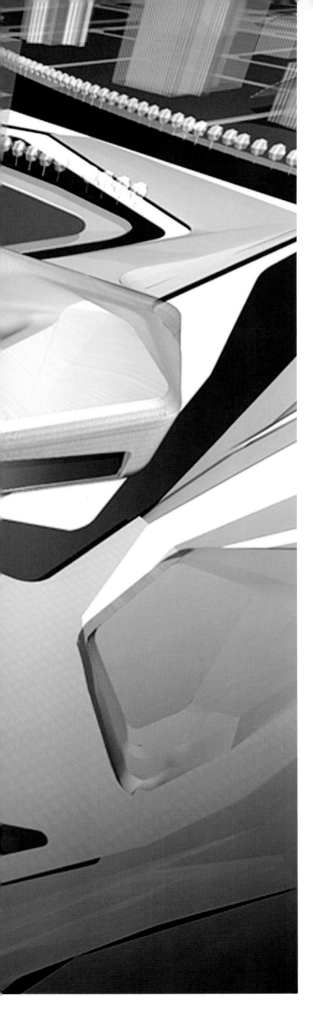

Guangzhou Opera House

Guangzhou 2005-

Architect Zaha Hadid

Zaha Hadid's view of architecture as 'object' is appropriate for the design of an opera house, where the building's external envelope can be moulded with freedom, while the internal performance spaces need to have their own envelopes, largely determined by acoustics. The classic example of this separation is the Sydney Opera House (1957-1973), where the outer envelopes are figurative while the inner envelopes (though not of Utzon's original design) define the performance spaces. The Baghdad-born London-based Hadid earned early fame with her victory in the international competition for the Hong Kong Peak Club in 1983. Seductive paintings show a 'horizontal skyscraper' (in her own words) hovering above an exaggerated mountainous Hong Kong landscape, like an alien spaceship landed from a science fiction film. Legend has it that juror Arata Isozaki picked it up from the dustbin, not unlike the apocryphal story of Eero Saarinen's selection of Utzon's discarded design for the Sydney Opera House competition.

2004 was an auspicious (in the Chinese manner) year for Hadid, winning the Guangzhou Opera House competition and architecture's 'Nobel Prize', the Pritzker. Again resembling alien objects that have landed from space, the symbolic reference for the Guangzhou Opera House is of 'worldly pebbles' washed smooth by Guangzhou's Pearl River. Unlike Sydney, where the harbour is the splendid setting for the opera house, Hadid has had to recreate a vast foreground, which she calls a 'desert', for the two entangled 'pebbles'. A computer rendered view (in place of the surreal acrylic paintings of Hadid's early career) from the gap between the two 'stones' is indeed intriguing... a vast 'desert' horizon is framed by the black and white stones. This image does makes one wonder why the opposite effect – two glossy pearls in a green landscape, perhaps more suitable for sub-tropical Guangzhou – was not chosen. Perhaps the English long for the desert from their lush island home, or perhaps the architect is nostalgic for her birthplace?

The organic shapes of Utzon's Sydney Opera House design have an undisputed geometry, with construction made possible by the assembly of prefabricated concrete ribs. The architect, in deriving geometric forms from a sphere, is now held in awe due to his ingenious artifice. On the other hand, the Guangzhou Opera House design – loosely following a self-entangled rising loop in each 'stone', which appears to respond to the shape of a theater in section – is by no means geometric. Alas, our ever-advancing supreme technology appears limitless in its capacity to erect structures in any form... so what now will be the artifice in architecture?

Left: The symbolic reference for the Guangzhou Opera House is of two 'worldly pebbles' washed smooth by the Pearl River.

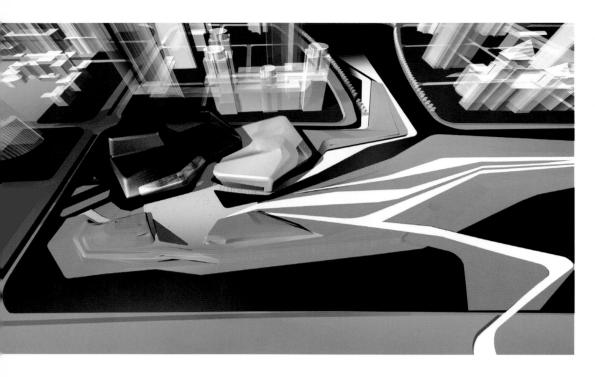

Left and below: The skyscrapers of Zhujiang New Town form a backdrop to the sculpted contours of the Opera House, which will provide a connection between the rapidly growing urban landscape and the riverfront.

Above: Interior views of the opera theater.

Shenzhen
Cultural Center

Shenzhen 1997-2005

Architect Arata Isozaki

As a city, Shenzhen is emphatic evidence of China's instant urbanization. In less than a decade, and blessed by the liberal economic policies specifically formulated for a series of 'special economic zones', a stretch of fishing villages on the border with Hong Kong was transformed into a modern city with a population of 1.5 million by the late 1980s. Its population is now estimated at 7 million. As it is increasingly becoming one of the nation's major economic centers, if not yet a cultural one, Shenzhen is keen to prove its maturity by building a grand and monumental urban center at the foot of Mount Lianhuashan, north of the city. Alongside the flamboyant new City Hall, which was built on an east-west axis, a cultural center has been placed on a north-south axis.

As any city that aspires to global status understands, economic capital must be transformed into cultural capital, which hopefully will become the measure of the sophistication of that city's cultural life. A universally recognized iconic building, as the Sydney Opera House has proved, may profoundly transform the city and its collective psyche. In 1997, Arata Isozaki won the international competition to build Shenzhen's (hopefully) iconic Cultural Center. In his long and fruitful architectural career, Isozaki's oeuvre appears to have recorded a chronological line of the architectural history of the second half of the 20th century. The Shenzhen Cultural Center, once again, proves that Isozaki's work is highly circumstantial... he is showing no sign of being vintaged.

The design needs no interpretation from a critic, for it is remarkably legible. A 300 meter-long and 40 meter-high black marble wall, which bounds the western edge of the complex, is broken in the middle to form a gateway to the urban center from the west, and it protects the complex from the heavily trafficked road. Service rooms are contained within the wall, and to its east, a library and two concert halls are housed in glass envelopes on the south and north blocks respectively. In addition to the undulating glass façade, which does not require much in the way of imagination to relate to music, the southern end of the library building has vertical and solid buildings radiating from it like an open book. Tree-like frames mark the entries for the library and the concert hall, which are finished with gilt: silver for the library and gold for the concert hall. One can safely assume this building will take no time to become popular among the citizens of Shenzhen, and its imitative character shall be quickly understood. But whether or not it will, like the Sydney Opera House, enshrine the imaginations of future generations, only time can tell. Nearly half a century after Jørn Utzon first designed the Sydney Opera House, the ingenious geometric solution to the fabrication of its structure, the laborious investment of mind, body, sweat, money and time, as well as its associated emotional and political vicissitudes, continue to intrigue... producing endless books, exhibitions and creative uses of its site as a public arena. In other words, this demonstrates a willingness from the citizens to engage with their building with imagination and loving care. This surely would not have come about if the Sydney Opera House had not been so defiantly conceived of as a time-honoured artifice.

Left: The undulating glass façade of the complex, viewed from the north east.

Above left: The concert hall lobby is marked with large tree-like frames.

Above right: The internal atrium space of the library.

Left: The tree-like frames in the library entry have a silver metallic appearance, in contrast to the warm golden hues of the concert hall lobby.

Right: Interior of a concert hall.

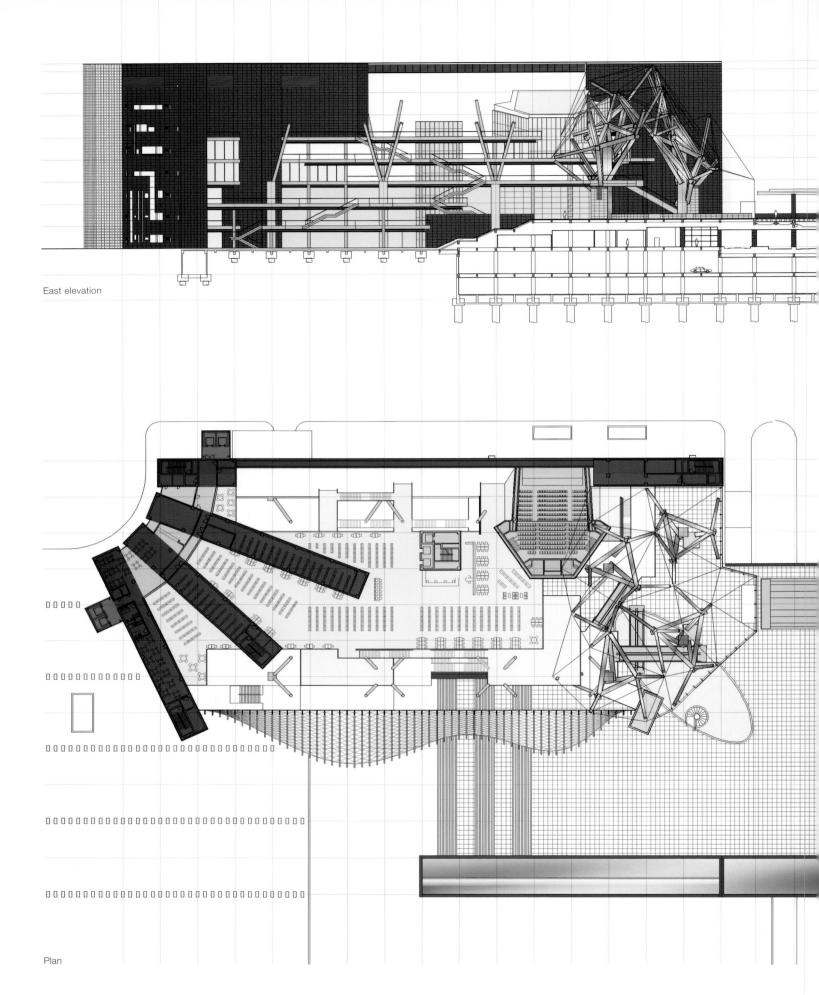

East elevation

Plan

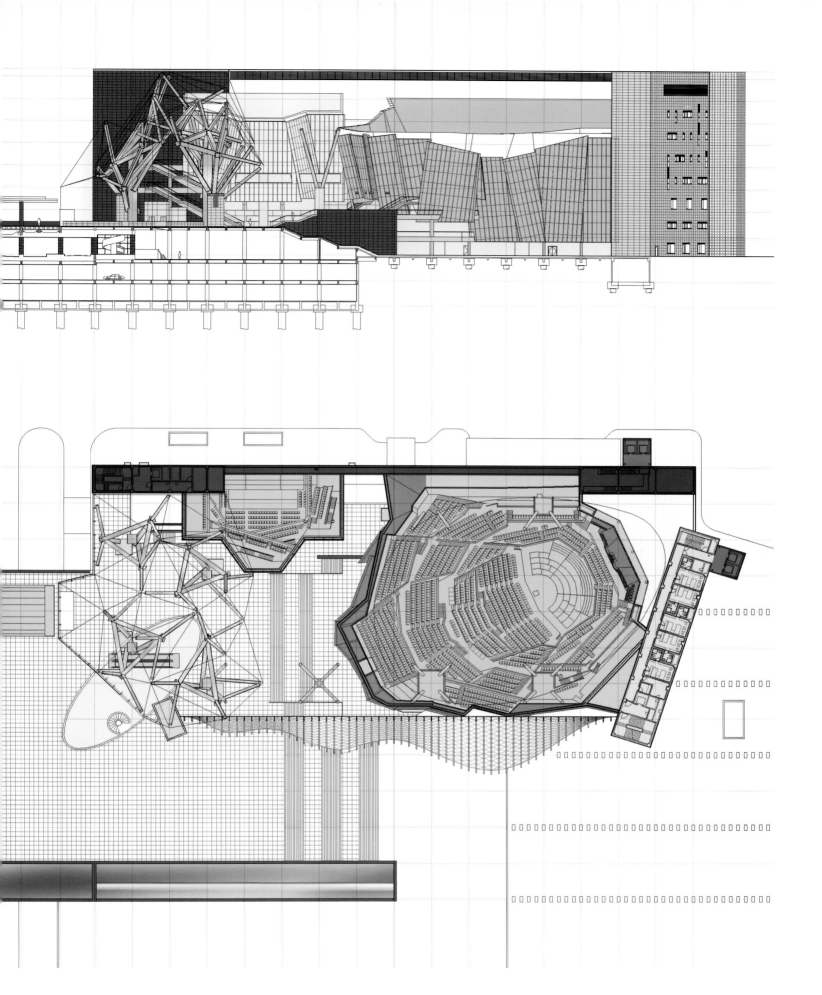

Faculty of Architecture and Civil Engineering, Shenzhen University

Shenzhen 2003

Architect Gong Weimin

In a period of twenty years, Shenzhen, a stretch of fishing villages near Hong Kong, has become a modern metropolis with a population of 7 million, and the Shenzhen University is as old as the urban history of Shenzhen. As early as in the mid 1980s, when 8 or 9 undergraduate students had to share one dormitory room in most Chinese universities, the campus of Shenzhen University, despite the 'infant' status of the university, was a much desired place, due to its modern facilities, and the generosity and freedom of space in its campus architecture. Even a shower in a dormitory room and stainless steel cutlery in the dining halls would impress any student from the interior provinces... the Shenzhen University campus stood for the hope of future Chinese universities. Twenty years later, the new complex for the Faculty of Architecture and Civil Engineering showcases the confidence and maturity of the young university.

The complex consists of three major components - teaching, practice and research - which is worth noting: this sort of integration is unexceptional in most Chinese universities, where practice and research are seen as integral parts of the professional disciplines, such as architecture and civil engineering. This does put many architecture and engineering schools in English speaking countries to shame, for in those countries, the professionals, academia and the other related disciplines most often remain secluded in their own 'silos'. The integration in this Shenzhen University faculty has reached an almost ideal level, one that even its Chinese counterparts cannot match. In China, for the university affiliated design institutes and the state-run design institutes, it is the norm to include architects and various engineers under one roof, but it is rare, even in China, to see architecture, planning and civil engineering taught within one building, as in Shenzhen. And furthermore, a library is included in the complex, and a publishing house for an architectural journal is accommodated in the research component. The architecture literally celebrates this integration by linking three major buildings together with open platforms, open courts, open corridors, flying bridges and internal atriums. All has been done with ease, as each component (a lecture theatre for example) announces its prominence through the façade, and they are all mostly connected by outdoor circulation spaces. The twenty-foot slope of the

Right: View from the north to the southern terrace of the faculty complex, showing the varied circulation links between the buildings.

214

site from north to south has been addressed by making the southern entry a grand terrace. The free spirit of a place like Shenzhen notwithstanding, the sub-tropical climate has indeed made it possible for the complex to be 'open'. No wonder Indian architect Charles Correa once went so far as suggesting that real architecture may be impossible outside the tropics. The architect for this faculty complex did not have to wrap the entire building with glass in order to make the building components and their institutional meanings externally 'readable': that, in Shenzhen's sub-tropical climate, would have been unfortunate.

The circulation links in this multidisciplinary faculty complex appear excessive in number and in floor area, but the architect wanted them to serve other purposes, such as taking a break from indoor rooms to enjoy campus and city views, and to stimulate accidental encounters with other people. This invitation to socializing in architecture has been extended to the interior, as each of the three 'buildings' has its own center: a three-storey atrium for the teaching building; a three-storey 'big studio' for the design institute; and a five-storey circulation court for the research building. Each of them, naturally, is connected to outdoor and other indoor social spaces. The grand atrium in the teaching building, for example, is ceremonially linked to the entry platform. Other social spaces, such as a 'jury hall' and a gallery (often sacrificed in other architecture schools due to economic rationalization on the part of the university management), further enhance a desired ambience of gregariousness in a multidisciplinary faculty.

The 'dialogues' between buildings, their connections via outdoor courts, corridors and bridges, as well as the horizontality that frames the views, will, according to the architect, evoke the feeling of a seamless relationship between indoor and outdoor spaces in pre-modern Chinese architecture. But isn't this feeling also universally desired?

Fourth floor plan

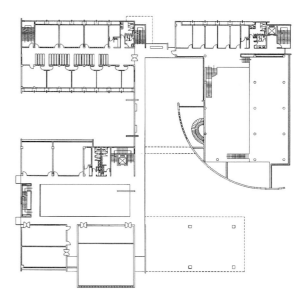

Third floor plan

Second floor plan

Left: The three major buildings of the complex are externally linked by open platforms, open courts and terraces, and flying bridges.

Above: View of the faculty from the east.

Right: Internal atriums connect the indoor and outdoor social spaces.

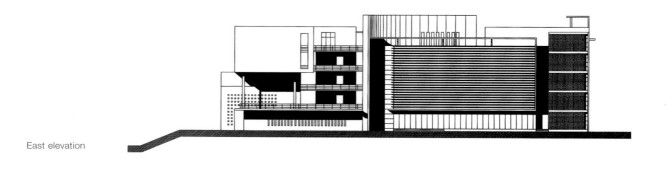

East elevation

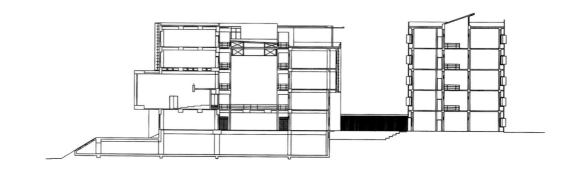

Section

Office of Planning and National Land Resources

Shenzhen 2001-2004

Architect Zhu Pei

In the 1980s, before China's modern and contemporary architecture received any international recognition, impatient young architectural students ventilated their dissatisfaction through criticism of the quasi-Beaux Arts method in China's architectural education, as they thought that the absence of early 20th century European Modernism in China would create an unbridgeable gap between Chinese architecture and that of Japan and the West. Japan's success, to the minds of young Chinese architects in the 1980s, was a result of its keen importation of European and American Modern architecture and education. It is no surprise that some of the most vocal voices of the 1980s have, since the late 1990s, begun to gain international attention through their architectural works in China. But it is perhaps to their surprise that 'sweet' recognition has arrived so easily, and that the 'gap' is not as large as they had once believed. Indeed, Zhu Pei's design for the Office of Planning and National Land Resources in Shenzhen is a competent piece of contemporary architecture by any international standard: it is sleekly modern with flexible open planning and transparency.

Flexible open planning and transparency now appear to frame the working life in a modern institution, and they have, to some degree, infiltrated private dwellings. But with a house or an apartment, the bedrooms and bathrooms, needless to say, are enclosed and 'fixed' as rooms. Open planning, arguably, counters the early modern belief of segregation in achieving hygiene and privacy. But one wonders what would be the real advantage to an institutional building if the notion of a room is completely dissolved into flexible open planning, within which circulation and usable space coexist as a continuous 'loop'? Despite the architect's efforts to design a steel frame 'flexible' office unit within the fixed concrete structure, there is a clear balance between the rooms and open spaces in the Shenzhen building: 'rooms' are enclosed on the north side, whereas the circulation spaces, generous in floor area and fully glazed, facilitate social interaction on the south. The transparency, achieved by the extensive use of glass, is according to the architect, more than a purely visual device: it has a symbolic role - that of democratic transparency - revealing the internal organization of a government institution to the Chinese public, who remain ambivalent about such democracy.

The building is well organized within its tight spatial disposition, it is well fabricated without the any sign of shoddy construction, and the use of deep windows on the northern façade complements the full glazing to the south. Other than the 'grounded' dining hall building

Left: The transparent and 'democratic' southern façade.

and car park, the office complex is 'lightly sited'. Due to its sophistication and contemporary aesthetic, this building would sit easily on any site, anywhere in the world. One wonders whether this 'universal fit' is result of our universal admiration of open flexible planning and transparency.

Two 20th century luminaries may shed some light on this issue: Mies van der Rohe and Louis Kahn, who represented two opposite positions. Kahn balanced rooms and open spaces, but Mies dissolved rooms to make flexible open plans. Kahn disliked glare: he was selective and cautious when admitting light, and used mainly masonry structures in his buildings. Mies, by contrast, was obsessed with glass and with the total transparency created by a fully glazed building, and he predominantly used steel frame structures. Kahn, paraphrasing an American poet, asked: "Which slice of the sun do you have in your building?" Mies, on the other hand, wished to reveal the skeleton of the building by using glass in place of outer walls, which for Mies would bring sufficient illumination to the interior, as well as a play of reflections (in his own words). So do open flexible planning and transparency mean the same thing for these two iconic architects? It would appear not. As the Miesian preference for open planning and transparency has been readily achieved by Chinese architects without going through decades of importation of modern architecture, will they now display enough confidence to site their building firmly in a place that may also embody the character of the institution that it accommodates?

Above: The circulation spaces on the southern side of the building, generous in floor area and fully glazed, facilitate social interaction.

Right: The use of deep windows on the northern façade complements the full glazing of the gently curved southern façade (far right).

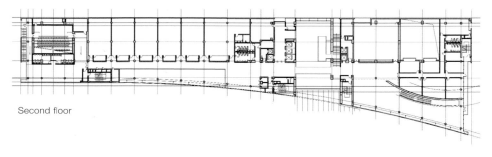

Second floor

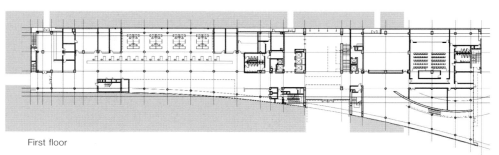

First floor

Above: The ground floor public areas on the southern edge of the building.

Right: The circulation corridor on the second floor runs over a bridge through the building's large entry atrium.

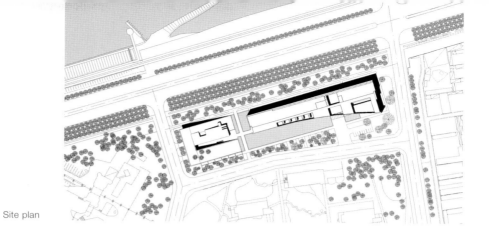

Site plan

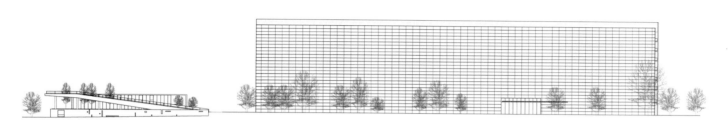

South elevation

North elevation

He Douling Studio

Chengdu 1995-1996

Architect Liu Jiakun

Unlike many of his Chinese contemporaries, Liu Jiakun does not rush to embrace the freedom of space, which is largely materialized in architecture as flexible open planning and transparency. This sense of freedom, however, has socio-cultural specificity with the new generation of Chinese architects, for it has only ruptured after nearly half a century of tight ideological control and a stagnant economy. Liu Jiakun's resistance to this seductive call for 'freedom' is noteworthy: he has always made solid buildings with limited openings, and he has always maintained the integrity of enclosed rooms within his buildings. Although he does not appear to refer to Louis Kahn or Luis Barragan in his verbalization of his own buildings, I count Liu Jiakun as one of their kindred spirits.

The studio and residence for sculptor He Douling is one of Liu Jiakun's early works, but it foreshadowed some common characteristics of his later works: a fortified bunker, the use of masonry, and a cubic form with selective openings. The spatial configuration of the He Douling Studio is simple - rooms wrap around a central court on two levels, with a curious diagonal ramp puncturing the enclosed cubic building from the east. The court, or 'patio' (as preferred by the architect), is not a 'sky well' predominantly for letting light into the rooms; the architect, rather unexpectedly, has inserted a 'chasm', filled by stairs, between the court and the rooms. As a result, the court, except for a low window on one side, is a walled room within which the sky is the ceiling. A single tree in this confined court charges it with Zen ambience: it demands meditation, but the tranquillity is brutally disturbed by the slanted flying bridge. This 'sudden turn', according to the architect, is Zen. As the Zen plot goes... the pupil asks the master "What is the meaning of cosmos?" The master says nothing, then all of a sudden, he slams his pupil on the face, and says "Go and sweep the courtyard!"

The court in this building is, as it demands, a room to heaven. The other rooms in this building, due to the 'chasm' that separates them from the court and sky light, are dark, and they are necessarily so. The openings, selective and sometimes one within the other, frame the landscape outside. They are indeed real windows, but what is a window? Qian Zhongshu, presumably not cognisant of the trend of using large areas of glass in Modern European architecture, had this to say in the 1930s...

It is spring again, windows can be opened more often. Spring sneaks in from the window, the man feels he can't stay in the room any longer - he walks out through the door. But the spring outside is too abundant! The glare is everywhere, but it is not as bright as that which penetrates the deep darkness of the room. The sun-baked wind seems to be lingering lazily everywhere, but it is not as delightful as that which disturbs the dullness of the room. Even the

Left: The fortified cubic form of sculptor He Douling's studio, viewed from the south east.

227

Right and below: A diagonal ramp punctures the cubic forms and selective openings. From within, the view of a single tree charges the space with *Zen* ambience.

North elevation

singing of the birds seems to be trifling and thin, it needs a background of silence from the interior of a room. We therefore understand that spring should be viewed from a window frame, just like a framed painting.

In the meantime, we feel that the window and the door have different meanings. A door, of course, is made to let people in and out, and a window can sometimes serve such a purpose. For example, a burglar, or the lover of a secret assignation, as in a novel, likes to climb through the window. The fundamental distinction between a window and a door is not merely determined as to whether or not people can be let in and out. Let's use the purpose of feeling spring, for argument's sake, where we might say that we can go out because there is a door; but we don't have to go out because there is a window.[1]

The artist stays in his room, and there really is no need for him to go out. Occasionally he may step into the 'room to heaven'… what more can he ask for?

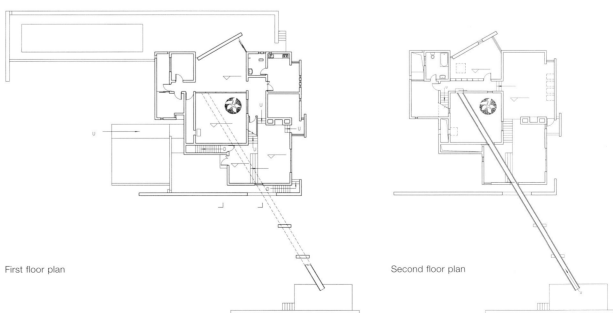

First floor plan   Second floor plan

Luyeyuan Stone Sculpture Museum

Chengdu 2001-2002

Architect Liu Jiakun

An art museum is a dream commission for architects, as it is not only the 'frame' for the artworks, but it can also be an artwork in itself. Arguably, a gallery should be neutral and subdued - in order not to compete with the art - but very few architects can resist the temptation, and consequently many of the well-known galleries in the world are destinations for architectural tourists. Liu Jiakun has handled this dilemma with a clever construction method - an inner layer of brick wall with an outer layer of *in situ* concrete - which enabled him to provide the usual internal white-washed neutral gallery space, but it is contained within an external concrete wall moulded by timber and slate. The idea, quite fittingly, was to imitate a piece of stone sculpture by using concrete as artificial stone, and the result is a monolithic, rough textured, concrete bunker with recessed vertical window slits.

The architect has been indulgent in further romanticizing the building's siting on a river: an artificial lotus pond was placed at the entry to the building, and a flying bridge ramp leads to the second level. The incline of the entry ramp is continued through the building onto a roof terrace, and the journey ends at a curious gazebo-like watchtower. It may well be that this roof terrace is the favourite place of the architect, as it is undecipherable, and a little mysterious. The gallery spaces are elegantly lit by vertical and horizontal slit openings, but they are expected rather than remarkable. It is the descending journey into the gallery from the second floor that makes the exhibition space feel like an 'underground' treasure house… the archetype of any museum.

This building has provoked much debate at a time when 'tectonics' is the buzzword among Chinese architects and students. Liu Jiakun has been accused of 'faking' the true brick wall and concrete structure frame by applying, from head to toe, a layer of concrete veneer. The architect has denied the decorative role of the concrete, as he sees the brick wall and concrete layer as symbiotic, both in terms of structure and method of construction. The brick wall was used as an inner layer of the *in situ* concrete mould during construction, which facilitated the concrete pouring for low-skilled builders, and was a convenient 'soft liner' (in the architect's own words) after completion for future modifications of electrical services. But no one seems to be curious about the 'dark side' of the architect, as evidenced by the strangely elevated gazebo on the roof terrace.

As one of the 'movers and shakers' in China's current architectural scene, Liu Jiakun is one of the few who never had a 'rite of passage' in the West. But as Louis Kahn said, some people, no matter what, simply know 'the blades of grass'.

Right: The gallery is entered by a flying ramp at second floor level.

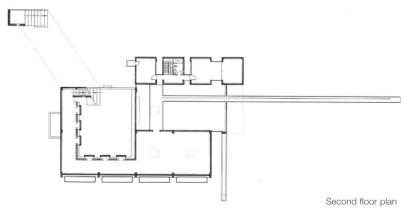

Second floor plan

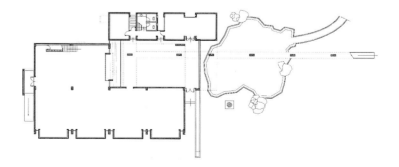

Above: The entry ramp leads over an artificial lotus pond to the second floor.

Left: The path through the building continues onto a roof terrace, with a curious gazebo-like watchtower.

First floor plan

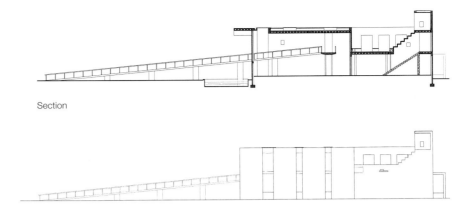

Section

South Elevation

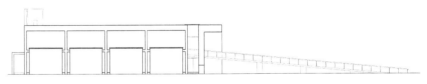

Section

Right: The museum, imitating a piece of stone sculpture, is a monolithic, rough textured, concrete bunker with recessed vertical window slits.

Below: The pathway leading to the museum's entry ramp… part of a journey that leads from the car park, through the forested grounds and the galleries, to the roof terrace.

North elevation

index

acknowledgments

This book grew out of a vision of Patrick Bingham-Hall, both in manner and matter, for which I have him to thank. I would like to acknowledge Huang Juzheng, who was the researcher for most part of the book; I have benefited not only from his access to the material, but also from his insights of the topic. Misunderstandings and errors, needless to say, remain my own. I am also grateful for the support of Professor John Ingleson and Professor Peter Murphy for a 'Contestable Grant' from the University of New South Wales, which enabled Huang Juzheng to work with me in Sydney for three months. Rachel Trigg and Christine Steinmetz were the enthusiastic readers of the earlier manuscripts; they offered suggestions more helpful than they know. Min-chia Young's skills assisted in the preparation of the manuscript. While witnessing an onslaught of building construction in Beijing, Professor Joseph Rykwert and Professor Jean-Louis Cohen offered timely encouragement for the lines of argument that I have tried to pursue in the book. Professor Yi-fu Tuan may not know that our conversations have provided assurance for my tangential thoughts. I owe great debts to Dongmin, whose 'no-problem-with-the-world' mentality resulted in Shumi and Shuyi's sense of humor, which sustained my frequent weekend absence when this small book was written.

Xing Ruan August 22, 2005

All drawings and computer images are supplied courtesy
of the architects for each project. The copyright for those
drawings and images resides with the architects.

OMA © – p2; 10; 56-61; 66-71
Kohn Pedersen Fox © – p10; 124-127
Steven Holl © – p11; 90-93
Paul Andreu © – p20; 46-51; 134-137
Foster and Partners © – p20; 21; 32-37; 146; 148-149
Zaha Hadid © – p20; 204-207
PTW Architects © – p21; 28; 72-77
Liu Jiakun © – p25; 228-229; 233-234
Yung Ho Chang, Atelier FCJZ © – p25; 79; 81
SOHO © – p25; 42; 96; 98; 100; 104-105; 108; 113;
117; 121; 122
Qi Xin © – p54-55
Wang Hui © – p88
Skidmore Owings and Merrill © – p128
Arte Jean-Marie Charpentier et Associés © – p141
Pei Cobb Freed and Partners © – p144-145
Zhang Bin and Zhou Wei, Tongji University Research and
Design Institute of Architecture © – p153; 156-157
Wu Jie and Tongji University Architectural Design Institute
© – p160
Wood and Zapata © – p164; 167
Zhang Zi and Zhang Ming, Original Design Studio © – p170
Wang Lu © – p176; 179
Wang Shu, Amateur Architectural Studio © – p180
MADA spam © – p184-187; 191-193; 196
Arata Isozaki © – p208-213
Gong Weimin © – p217-218
Zhu Pei © – p224-225

All photography © by Patrick Bingham-Hall
except as listed below:

Page 15, figures 2 and 3: from © Yang Tingbao Jianzhu
Sheji Zuoping
Page 17, figure 6: from © Yang Tingbao Jianzhu Sheji Zuoping
Page 45, right center and right bottom: courtesy © SOHO
Page 149, top left and above right: courtesy © Foster and
Partners. Photographer: Kerun Ip

Patrick Bingham-Hall would like to thank Huang Juzheng for
his coordination of transport, his introductions to the architects
and for obtaining permission to photograph many of the
projects throughout China. Many thanks as well to Yue Ziqing
and Shan Hao for their assistance in Shenzhen.